I0003136

First Steps in
SAP® Fiori

Anurag Barua

Thank you for purchasing this book from Espresso Tutorials!

Like a cup of espresso coffee, Espresso Tutorials SAP books are concise and effective. We know that your time is valuable and we deliver information in a succinct and straightforward manner. It only takes our readers a short amount of time to consume SAP concepts. Our books are well recognized in the industry for leveraging tutorial-style instruction and videos to show you step by step how to successfully work with SAP.

Check out our YouTube channel to watch our videos at *https://www.youtube.com/user/EspressoTutorials*.

If you are interested in SAP Finance and Controlling, join us at *http://www.fico-forum.com/forum2/* to get your SAP questions answered and contribute to discussions.

Related titles from Espresso Tutorials:

- ▶ Dominique Alfermann, Stefan Hartmann, Benedikt Engel: SAP® HANA Advanced Modeling
  http://5110.espresso-tutorials.com
- ▶ Christian Savelli: SAP® BW on SAP HANA
  http://5128.espresso-tutorials.com
- ▶ Janet Salmon & Claus Wild: First Steps in SAP® S/4HANA Finance
  http://5149.espresso-tutorials.com
- ▶ Bert Vanstechelman: The SAP® HANA Deployment Guide
  http://5171.espresso-tutorials.com

Table of Contents

Anurag Barua
First Steps in SAP® Fiori

ISBN: 978-1-51204-134-7

Editor: Tracey Duffy

Cover Design: Philip Esch

Cover Photo: fotolia #78749435 | Romolo Tavani

Interior Design: Johann-Christian Hanke

All rights reserved.

1st Edition 2017, Gleichen

© 2017 by Espresso Tutorials GmbH

URL: *www.espresso-tutorials.com*

All rights reserved. Neither this publication nor any part of it may be copied or reproduced in any form or by any means or translated into another language without the prior consent of Espresso Tutorials GmbH, Zum Gelenberg 11, 37130 Gleichen, Germany.

Espresso Tutorials makes no warranties or representations with respect to the content hereof and specifically disclaims any implied warranties of merchantability or fitness for any particular purpose. Espresso Tutorials assumes no responsibility for any errors that may appear in this publication.

Feedback
We greatly appreciate any kind of feedback you have concerning this book. Please mail us at *info@espresso-tutorials.com*.

The SAP eBook Library: Team and Company Access

Did you know that you can provide your team with effective SAP training with access to the SAP eBook Library and reduce travel and training costs? You can!

Curious about how we stack up against the competition?

	Espresso Tutorials	Other Offerings
Price per Year	**$159 annually**	**$1599 annually**
SAP eBooks	✓	✗
SAP video tutorials	✓	✓
Mobile app	✓	✓
Immediate access to new titles	✓	✓
Self service to maintain users (for companies)	✓	✓

Pricing available for teams of 5+. A team of 10 can access the library for one year for $1390 (pre-tax). The larger your team, the more you save.

Try a free 7-day, no-obligation trial:
http://free.espresso-tutorials.com

Get a quote for your team today:
http://company.espresso-tutorials.com

Introduction

In the realm of software called *Enterprise Resource Planning (ERP)*, SAP has been the leader and flag-bearer for over 40 years, offering an "engine" that has consistently represented the highest degree of engineering excellence. However, the user interface and the overall user experience in an SAP system have always been an afterthought. The development of these aspects has been a very long learning experience and a process of evolution in the mindset of the strategists at SAP. The process has been aided by many technological advances in user interfaces that have seen the user experience make the journey from function keys on the keyboard to the world-class experience of SAP Fiori.

I feel that we have arrived at an inflection point in the evolution of both SAP as a company and SAP as a software suite. While the company has established solid foundations with the strength of its engineering, further augmented by HANA, it is the (satisfying) user experience that both existing and new users will expect and sometimes demand as part of their overall SAP experience. SAP Fiori is intended to be the answer to those demands.

It is an honor and a pleasure for me to combine eighteen years of being part of the SAP ecosystem with my passion for a great end user experience in order to write this short book on SAP Fiori. If you are just getting started on your SAP Fiori odyssey, this book should be a good starting point for you. It is aimed at anyone who is interested in SAP Fiori—regardless of whether you are an analyst, developer, manager, sales engineer, or an executive.

I hope that you enjoy the book and it helps you to get started on your own SAP Fiori journey after reading it.

We have added a few icons to highlight important information. These include:

Tip

Tips highlight information concerning more details about the subject being described and/or additional background information.

Example

Examples help illustrate a topic better by relating it to real world scenarios.

Attention

Attention notices highlight information that you should be aware of when you go through the examples in this book on your own.

Finally, a note concerning the copyright: all screenshots printed in this book are the copyright of SAP SE. All rights are reserved by SAP SE. Copyright pertains to all SAP images in this publication. For the sake of simplicity, we do not mention this specifically underneath every screenshot.

1 History of end user experience with SAP

Let me begin this book with a short anecdote. There was once a guy, let's call him Alex, who loved fast cars and wanted to own one. Unfortunately, he didn't have the money to buy such a car. After working really hard for many years and saving aggressively, he had enough money to buy a Ferrari. He went to his local Ferrari dealership and started talking to a car salesperson. Alex had always been obsessed with the engine and that's what he told the salesperson. The salesperson tried to coax him into exploring the incredible interiors, all the gadgetry, navigation features, and the works, but Alex kept reminding him of his only interest: the engine. Somewhat exasperated, the salesperson took Alex to the showroom, where he showed him a couple of models that had only a chassis. He handed Alex the keys to one of the models for a test drive. A nonplussed Alex asked the salesperson how he was supposed to drive a car that had only an engine but no way to communicate with the engine. The salesperson responded that they believed in selling a user experience and not just the engine, and the user experience was part of the package Alex would be paying for.

The moral of the story: anything mechanical, whether it is an automobile or a software application, needs a user interface that conceals the underlying complexity of the object in question and entices the operator or user to communicate with it in an efficient and satisfying manner.

1.1   History of input devices and user interfaces

I will start this book by going back in time to share with you the history of user interfaces in general and in SAP software in particular. This will help you to understand the role SAP Fiori will play in SAP's *user experience (UX)* strategy and the evolution of user interfaces at SAP.

In the early days of mainframes, computers were not unlike turbines and generators that take input and convert it into utilitarian output. What the computers could do or generate was far more important than how easy it was to enter the input. In fact, around the time that the initial seeds of SAP were sown and starting to germinate, punch cards were the most reliable and popular way of entering data into computers. Punched tapes appeared alongside punch cards and were an offshoot of the textile industry. For those of you who are too young to remember or were possibly not even born then, it seems unbelievable that around only four decades ago, punches or holes in each column of a punched card represented one alphanumeric character. And in terms of instructing the computer to execute a command (imagine a line of code in a programming language such as Fortran), each card represented one line of code. Mainframe computers were workhorses that worked behind the scenes to simplify and expedite complex tasks for entities that were able to afford these behemoths. As such, it was only a small group of people (primarily programmers) that really needed to operate these computers. Not surprisingly, the concept of the user interface—as we understand it today—did not exist.

Obviously, this way of interacting with computers was not going to continue for too long and someone was going to come up with a new idea that would eventually go mainstream. That idea was the *keyboard*. It was not a radical idea because the computer keyboard was modeled on the standard typewriter keyboard. This mode of data entry has weathered all kinds of technological storms and to this day, is still the most popular global medium for data entry. Using the keyboard as a peripheral data input device made great sense as mainframe computers became more commonplace and companies started to build applications that ultimately needed the user to provide direct input.

In the early 1980s, as the *personal computer (PC)* revolution took off, the *graphical user interface (GUI)* dethroned the by now clunky character-based interfaces as the de facto standard. This transition was accelerated by the growing footprint of Microsoft Windows-based computing. It is interesting to note here that the GUI was more of an Apple innovation than a Microsoft one, but the latter made it truly mainstream while Apple and its desktops were perceived as upscale machines for artists, designers, desktop publishers, etc. rather than a medium for the masses. While a keyboard and a character-based user interface seemed like a match made in heaven, a keyboard did not necessarily seem like a good fit for a GUI. The need for greater convenience and flexibility in navigating through graphical elements seemed more suited to a *point-and-click* interface. Enter the *mouse*.

Here's an interesting fact about the mouse: as a tool, the mouse was originally invented in the early 1960s but was relegated to the realm of intellectual curiosity in its early years. However, as Xerox and Apple started realizing its value in the 1970s (in perfect cadence with the PC revolution that was well underway at that time), the mouse started appearing with many PCs worldwide. And after Microsoft jumped onto the bandwagon and understood the power of the relatively inexpensive rubber ball, the mouse was well on its way to becoming as ubiquitous in a PC environment as a salt shaker is on a family dinner table—as it still is to this day.

Meanwhile, the computing world started to move away from PCs towards laptops and a variety of mobile devices (including the once wildly popular *personal digital assistants (PDAs)*), *tablets*, and *smartphones*. Add to that the tremendous strides made with touch-screen computing in the last 10 years or so, combined with the increasing popularity of voice-recognition technologies such as Apple's Siri, Microsoft's Cortana, and many more, and you can see that peripherals such as the keyboard and the mouse are on the path to obsolescence.

Internet of Things

Today, in the era of connectedness, multiple devices per person, and the advent of the Internet of Things (IoT), the need for a satisfying user experience is paramount. Every company that has been around for as long as SAP has had to reinvent itself on various fronts. Traditionally, the user experience with SAP has been less than satisfying. SAP Fiori represents a major leap in the direction of the reinvention of the SAP user experience.

1.2 SAP and the user interface

Since its inception in 1972, SAP has undergone a long and fascinating journey: a journey that has seen the world go from mainframe computers that required incredible amounts of floor space to miniature devices that have considerably more processing capacity than the mainframes. Even a good 15 years after SAP had been in business, the term *Internet* had not even been coined.

1.2.1 SAP GUI in R/1

Let us look at the one of the earliest incarnations of the SAP GUI. This was in the early days of SAP, in the early 1970s to be precise, and was part of the first major integrated suite of business functions of SAP: R/1. Figure 1.1 shows a typical R/1 user interface screen.

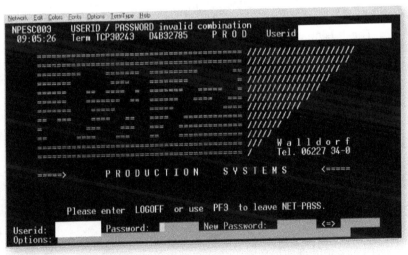

Figure 1.1: The earliest version of an SAP GUI (source: https://prezi.com/gzx78ax-c1p1/evolution-of-sap-gui/)

Anyone who has ever laid their hands on mainframes such as PDP-11 will recognize the non-graphical terminal-based data entry screen. All the navigation was through the keyboard. You had to use the *tab* key extensively to jump from one data entry field to the other. The screen also required extensive use of the function buttons on the keyboard. Remember also that the mouse was an item that was in the realm of the exotic if not necessarily in the science fiction domain. So even though it seems unbelievable today, this earliest version of the SAP GUI did not involve the mouse as a means of navigation.

1.2.2   SAP GUI in R/2

As SAP started acquiring a bigger user base and becoming more integrated with the dominant technological standards of the 1970s, the need for an improved GUI became more pronounced. In the late 1970s, SAP launched its next integrated suite of applications in R/2. The business capabilities of this software were accompanied by a new version of the GUI.

This new version of the SAP GUI was not vastly different to its predecessor from the perspective of an end user experience. However, there were quite a few new features such as a list of function keys at the bottom of the screen and a more menu-driven approach to make navigation smoother.

1.2.3   SAP GUI in R/3

In 1992, after 20 years of existence, SAP reached adulthood in more senses than one. The transition from mainframe to client-server finally took place with the advent of the R/3 era. This fundamental switch from mainframe to client-server came with the concept of the *client* computer. The term *front-end* entered the lexicon. For a short time, the personal computer (PC) revolution had kicked into high gear and users worldwide were starting to enjoy this new experience of this thing called the graphical user interface, or GUI, epitomized by Apple's OSF/Motif and Microsoft's Windows operating systems. SAP could therefore no longer continue to offer its character-based user interface to its exploding customer base.

Therefore, SAP started shipping its OSF/Motif-based GUI. Looking back, it would be hard to categorize this product as a GUI. It had hardly any of the traditional components that one would expect in a GUI, such as radio buttons and checkboxes. Frankly, it was merely a slightly improved version of the R/2 user interface. The R/3 interface is shown in Figure 1.2.

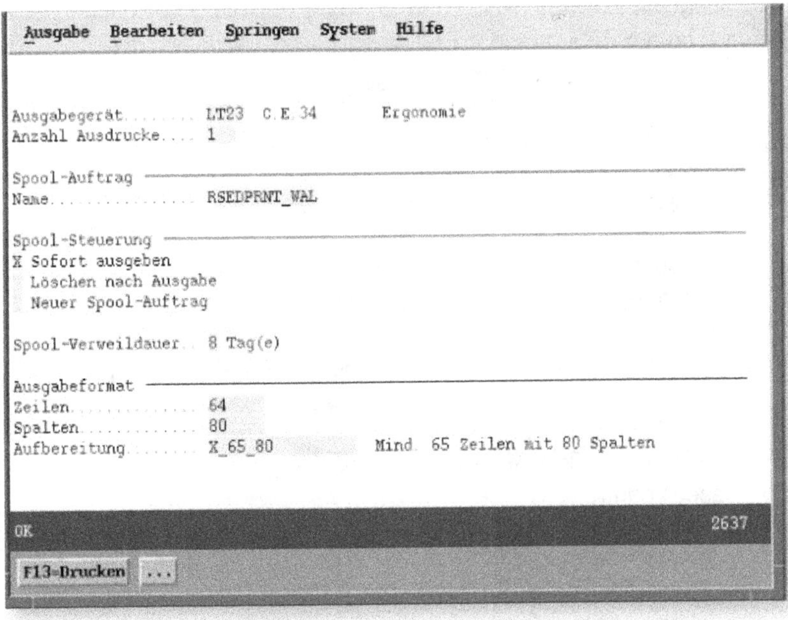

Figure 1.2: SAP GUI in R/3 (source: https://prezi.com/gzx78ax-c1p1/evolution-of-sap-gui/)

Unfortunately, this screenshot is available only in German. However, you can see that it provided users with a menu bar at the top and also a pushbutton at the bottom.

17

1.2.4 The evolution of the SAP GUI through the 1990s

Over the next few years, SAP made many improvements and as more and more big corporations started implementing SAP, and the era of personal computing made its inexorable march, further improvements were made to the GUI. Because the popularity of PCs was driven largely by the user-friendly GUI that was now almost synonymous with Microsoft Windows, SAP added key elements of Windows (such as checkboxes, radio buttons, pushbuttons, etc.) to its interface to impart a heavy Windows-like feel. And soon enough, the Windows GUI became SAP's standard GUI. This was officially called Version 2.

Additional improvements resulted in Version 3 of the SAP GUI, which was released in 1995. The controls in this version had an even greater Windows feel to them.

Version 4 of the SAP GUI hit the market in 1998. This version was more streamlined. Tabs were provided in transactions in order to reduce the number of screens a user would have to navigate through within a transaction.

The next version (4.5) introduced many new (ActiveX-based) controls.

With the release of R/3 version 4.6c in early 2001 (the next version of the SAP GUI (4.6)), the GUI was extensively revamped and had a different look and feel. It was designed to improve the overall user experience and productivity. The screens became more self-contained. The design philosophy was to prevent users having to exit a screen. Tree controls were therefore incorporated into a lot of complex transactions (such as the sales order and purchase order creation transactions). This version of the GUI represented SAP's well-intentioned effort to improve the overall user experience and also standardize the look and feel across different platforms. Therefore, the GUI had a less Windows-like look and feel than its predecessors. The concept behind this paradigm was called Frog GUI. A typical SAP transaction screen based on this paradigm is shown in Figure 1.3.

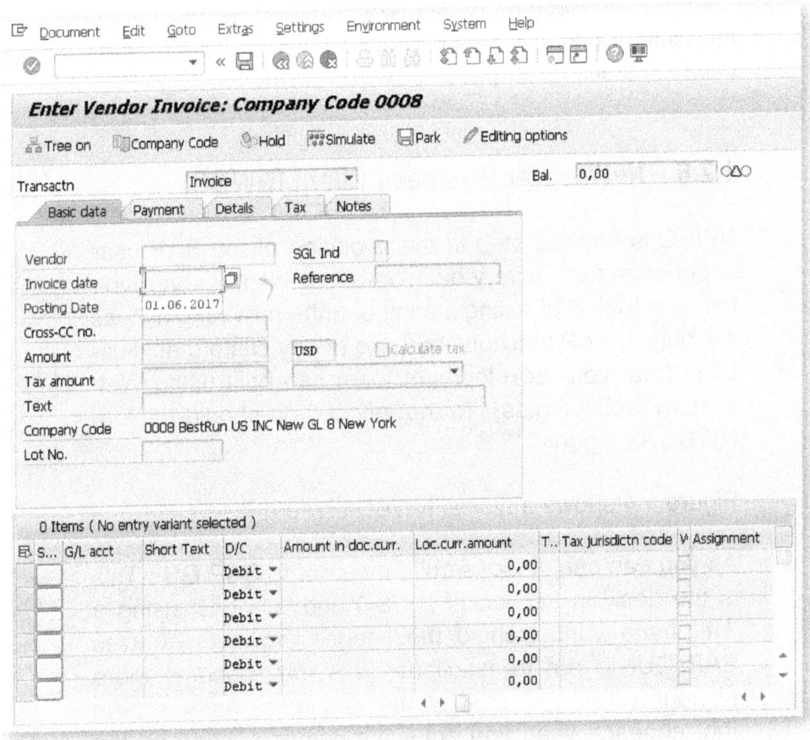

Figure 1.3: Typical SAP transaction screen based on the Frog GUI paradigm

1.2.5   The SAP GUI in the Enterprise R/3 and NetWeaver era

SAP moved to a new era of Enterprise R/3 with the release of version 4.7 in 2003. This was necessitated by the explosive growth of the Internet as the medium for both commerce and user interaction. Another driver for this version was the growing popularity of *service-oriented architecture (SOA)*. SAP therefore designed a technology platform called NetWeaver and the new application stack (Enterprise R/3) ran on top of it.

1.2.6   NetWeaver Business Client (NWBC)

NWBC is another step in the evolution of the SAP user experience from a very desktop-based client-server type mindset to that of a single point of entry providing access not only to SAP functions but also to any custom applications (that your development team has built using Web Dynpro technologies). To that effect, you should think of NWBC as a portal.

Figure 1.4 shows a typical NWBC screen.

As you can see, it looks quite different to SAP GUI. This is the desktop version of NWBC and it is built using a .Net framework. Behind the scenes, however, it uses SAP GUI to run transactions. This may become more obvious when you look at the document entry screen that appears when you enter the company code on the screen shown above. Figure 1.5 shows a G/L account document screen in NWBC.

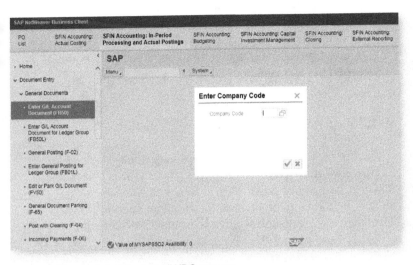

Figure 1.4: A typical NWBC screen

Figure 1.5: G/L account document entry screen in NWBC

There are a lot of features that hark back to SAP GUI. However, you will see a lot of other user-friendly features—especially the function buttons and their placement—that show that this is an improved and more user-friendly interface than SAP GUI.

While this may not be particularly important to you, there is another (light) version of NWBC called NWBC for HTML. As a user, you will detect hardly any differences between the two versions.

1.2.7 And finally, today...

On the previous few pages, I have very briefly explained how SAP has evolved in its approach to user experience since its earliest days. This indeed has been an evolution, a journey over several decades that span the whole gamut of technological advances that SAP has had to either keep pace with or be at the cutting edge of.

Today, SAP is at the bleeding edge of providing its global user base with a satisfying user experience. Hence, in addition to all the traditional modes of user interaction with SAP's applications, we now have SAP Fiori. Although the subsequent chapters are devoted to SAP Fiori, there is one thing I would like to make clear at this early stage: SAP Fiori manifests SAP's most advanced thinking on what an intuitive, user-friendly, and productivity-boosting user experience should look and feel like.

2 What ails traditional SAP user interfaces?

Initially, I wanted to call this chapter "What ails SAP GUI?" because SAP GUI is synonymous with SAP user interfaces. SAP GUI is used by millions of users spanning companies of all sizes, straddling all kinds of industries, and across all continents. It is therefore one of the most widely used and recognized user interfaces in the world. There are others, such as Web GUI, NetWeaver Business Client, etc. However, these other technologies generally fall within the "Plan B" or "Plan C" realm and SAP GUI is considered the default interface.

To return to my question: using SAP GUI as the primary manifestation of the SAP user interface, let us take a look at its less pleasing aspects:

▶ For any standard transaction such a purchase order, sales order, invoice, etc., the standard SAP screens contain hundreds of fields, many of which are of little to no relevance to a user.

▶ The number of tabs and fields leads to excessive clicking or navigation, which is not productive.

▶ The options for customizing/personalizing these screens are not straight-forward or easy for the casual user. In some cases, coding is required to customize the screens, which is not something you can expect from even a power user.

▶ The overall user experience with SAP GUI is generally considered to be less than pleasant.

This is a statement that I have been hearing for many, many years, even when "user experience" was not as prominent a factor as it is today. Dark gray screens have become synonymous with SAP GUI and for years, users have been complaining about the unsatisfactory experience. Although this is a qualitative assessment, it is hard to argue with it.

▶ There is no direct way to access SAP GUI via mobile devices. Suffice to say, SAP GUI was conceived long before mobile computing became the craze it is today.

2.1 An illustration of interaction with SAP GUI

I will now take you through the steps of creating a purchase order (PO) using the standard SAP GUI interface to illustrate the points made above.

2.1.1 The purchase order user interface in SAP GUI

To illustrate the need for a more simplified user interface, let's take a look at one of the most popular SAP transactions—creating a purchase order (transaction ME21N). A standard purchase order has two major components: a header and line item(s). Let us look at the header section first. Figure 2.1 shows the initial PO header screen in an ERP 6.0 system running on SAP GUI 7.40.

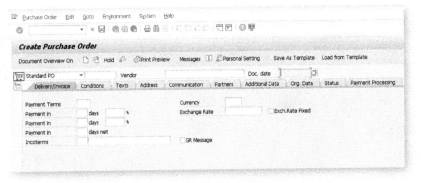

Figure 2.1: PO header screen in an ERP 6.0 system

While it may not be immediately obvious, the header section has 10 tabs each with a large number of fields. Figure 2.1 shows the fields on the DELIVERY/INVOICE tab. Now let's take a peek at the next tab, TEXTS.

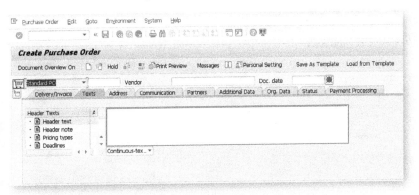

Figure 2.2: TEXTS tab in the PO creation transaction

Figure 2.3 shows the third tab, CONDITIONS.

Figure 2.3: CONDITIONS tab in the PO creation transaction

Let us now move to the fourth tab, ADDRESS, as shown in Figure 2.4. As you can see, there are a lot of fields for entering data pertaining to the address of the vendor.

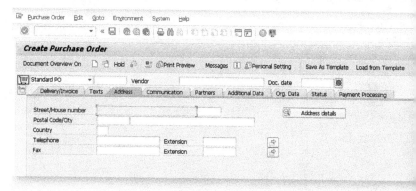

Figure 2.4: ADDRESS tab in the PO creation transaction

Figure 2.5 shows the fifth tab, COMMUNICATION. This tab contains five fields for data entry related to how you communicate with your vendor.

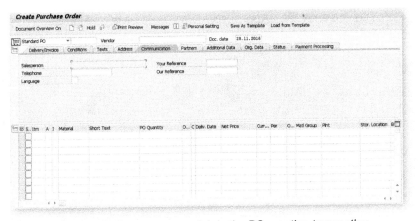

Figure 2.5: COMMUNICATION tab in the PO creation transaction

We now move on to the next tab, PARTNERS, as shown in Figure 2.6.

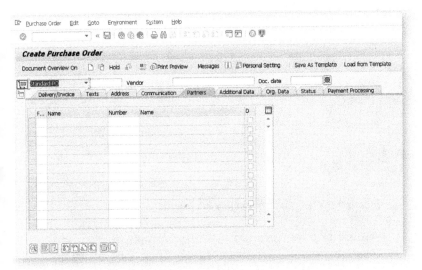

Figure 2.6: PARTNERS tab in the PO creation transaction

The seventh tab, ADDITIONAL DATA is shown in Figure 2.7.

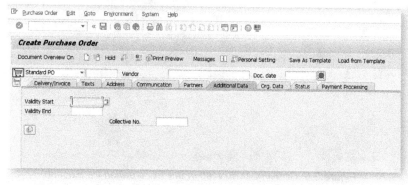

Figure 2.7: ADDITIONAL DATA tab in the PO creation transaction

Our PO creation/journey is not yet complete but we are close. Let's now shift our attention to the ORG. DATA tab shown in Figure 2.8.

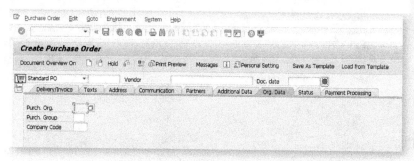

Figure 2.8: ORG. DATA tab in the PO creation transaction

We will skip the next tab, STATUS, because you do not need to enter any data here. This tab contains informational data. Let's finish our journey by looking at the contents of the tab on the far right-hand side, PAY-MENT PROCESSING. This is shown in Figure 2.9.

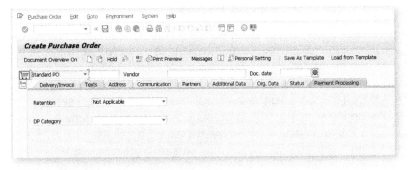

Figure 2.9: PAYMENT PROCESSING tab in the PO creation transaction

Wait, we are not done. All the tabs that we have discussed thus far relate merely to the header of the PO. Each PO will have one or more line items. Let's now move to the PO items screen. Figure 2.10 shows part of this screen.

Figure 2.10: PO line item entry

As you might infer from the horizontal scroll bar, there is a long list of fields that are available for data input. Each line item has specific items of information related directly to the item you are ordering, such as the quantity, net price, delivery date, etc.

2.2 What does this all mean?

Why did I take you through all these screens? If you have never seen and/or posted a basic transaction such as a PO in an SAP system, this brief journey has hopefully given you a sense of the overwhelming user experience doing so can present. In fact, the first time I ran this transaction, I was overwhelmed by all the many things you can do. While the versatility of every SAP business transaction is impressive, you may well ask what happens if you really need just a very few fields to complete the transaction. If you are new to the SAP world and have come from a world where such transactions are very intuitive and require minimal data entry with just a few clicks, having to navigate through so many screens could be a big deterrent to using SAP. This is a challenge that businesses worldwide have been grappling with ever since they started using SAP.

If you count up the available fields at the header and item levels, to the result is hundreds of fields. Although only some of these fields are mandatory, you often have to "enter" or "tab" your way past what seems like an endless number of fields which may mean very little to you (if anything) and often a whole number of warning and information messages that also may mean very little to you. And the whole time, you are dealing with a user interface that is not very appealing. This could be a significant barrier to entry—in fact, it has been for a long time.

What if the process of creating a purchase order in your organization is straight-forward? What if you only need to enter information in four or five fields? Obviously, having to navigate past so many fields and messages is not very productive. Let's take a look at a specific example. If we assume that POs in your organization are created without any conditions, why would this tab even have to be displayed? And even if it is available, would it be possible to hide it? Now what if most of your purchase orders need to be entered via a mobile device? As you may know, things can become even more complicated here if you are expecting the SAP GUI to render the user interface on a mobile device exactly as you would expect it to. What if you simply do not like the SAP GUI from an aesthetic standpoint and you are looking for a more appealing, user-friendly, and intutive user interface?

One of the ways that you can bridge all these gaps is by personalizing the end user experience. In Chapter 3, I will discuss the concept of personalization in SAP systems and the methods that are available to you to do this. From what I have discussed so far, you would be correct to think of SAP Fiori as (currently) the culmination of the efforts by SAP to provide a very high level of personalization.

3 Personalization in SAP systems

What is personalization? It is the possibility for users to tailor aspects of their interaction with a software application to most efficiently meet their specific behavior and habits. At the end of Chapter 2, I posed a few questions. SAP has tried to answer each of these questions by providing individual workarounds or solutions, all of which can be addressed using personalization. The ability to customize the nature of a field from a data input perspective (i.e., whether a field is mandatory or optional) has been part of the standard SAP configuration (the Implementation Guide (IMG) menu) since the early years of SAP. It is available for almost every module in SAP. Furthermore, the idea of bundling the input/output behavior of a set of fields into a *field status variant* and then assigning the field status variant to a fundamental component, such as a company code or a cost center (in the case of Financial Accounting), is very common in SAP. The following is an illustration of how you can do this for Financial Accounting in the IMG.

3.1 Personalization: An example

Figure 3.1 shows the navigation path for defining field status variants in the IMG (FINANCIAL ACCOUNTING • FINANCIAL ACCOUNTING GLOBAL SETTINGS • DOCUMENT • LINE ITEM • CONTROLS • DEFINE FIELD STATUS VARIANTS).

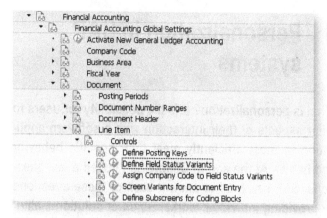

Figure 3.1: Defining field status variants in the IMG

When you click the IMG activity highlighted in Figure 3.1, the list of existing field statuses appears. This is shown in Figure 3.2.

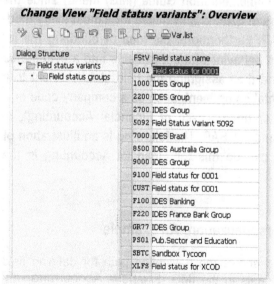

Figure 3.2: Existing field status variants

Let's take a look at field status variant 0001. Select field status **0001** and then click FIELD STATUS GROUPS in the DIALOG STRUCTURE pane on the left to go to the next screen. Let's take a look at field status group **G004** (cost accounts). This is shown in Figure 3.3.

Field status group	Text
G001	General (with text, allocation)
G003	Material consumption accounts
G004	Cost accounts
G005	Bank accounts (obligatory value date)
G006	Material accounts
G007	Asset accts (w/o accumulated depreciatn)
G008	Assets area clearing accounts
G009	Bank accounts (obligatory due date)
G011	Clearing accounts (with settlement per.)
G012	Receivables/payables clearing
G013	General (obligatory text)
G014	MM adjustment accounts
G017	Freight/customs provisions/clearing (MM)
G018	Scrapping (MM)
G019	Other receivables/payables
G023	Plant maintenance accounts
G025	Inventory adjustment accounts
G026	Accounts for down payments made
G029	Revenue accounts
G030	Change in stock accounts

Dialog Structure
▼ Field status variants
  · Field status groups

Field status variant   0001   Field status for 0001

Figure 3.3: Field status groups available for field status variant 0001

Now double-click group **G004** to display the screen shown in Figure 3.4.

Because we are interested in maintaining the behavior of fields in payment transactions, double-click PAYMENT TRANSACTIONS. On the next screen, you can change the input/output nature of the fields that belong to this group. This is shown in Figure 3.5.

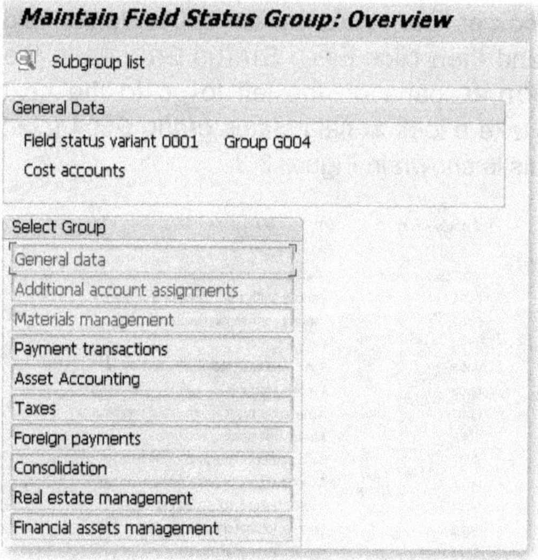

Maintain Field Status Group: Overview

🔍 Subgroup list

General Data

Field status variant 0001   Group G004
Cost accounts

Select Group

General data
Additional account assignments
Materials management
Payment transactions
Asset Accounting
Taxes
Foreign payments
Consolidation
Real estate management
Financial assets management

Figure 3.4: Selecting the relevant group for customizing

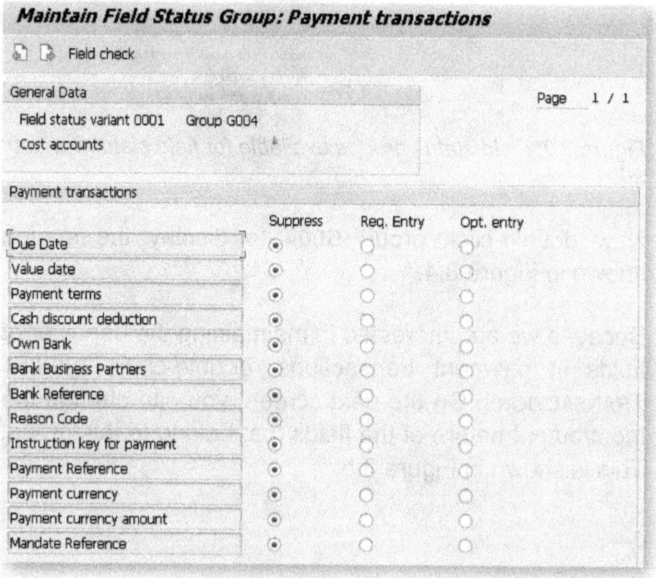

Maintain Field Status Group: Payment transactions

📄 📄 Field check

General Data   Page   1 / 1

Field status variant 0001   Group G004
Cost accounts

Payment transactions

	Suppress	Req. Entry	Opt. entry
Due Date	◉	○	○
Value date	◉	○	○
Payment terms	◉	○	○
Cash discount deduction	◉	○	○
Own Bank	◉	○	○
Bank Business Partners	◉	○	○
Bank Reference	◉	○	○
Reason Code	◉	○	○
Instruction key for payment	◉	○	○
Payment Reference	◉	○	○
Payment currency	◉	○	○
Payment currency amount	◉	○	○
Mandate Reference	◉	○	○

Figure 3.5: Changing the status of fields within a field status group

You can now control whether you want each field to be a required entry field, an optional field, or whether the field should be hidden/supresssed in the specific SAP transaction. Finally, you have to assign the company code to the field status variant (containing the field groups that you have changed). In the IMG, navigate as follows to the relevant activity (shown in Figure 3.6): FINANCIAL ACCOUNTING • FINANCIAL ACCOUNTING GLOBAL SETTINGS • DOCUMENT • LINE ITEM • CONTROLS • ASSIGN COMPANY CODE TO FIELD STATUS VARIANTS.

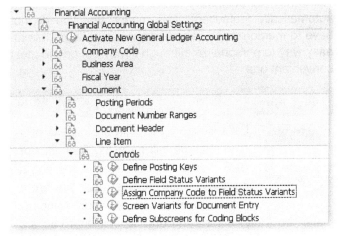

Figure 3.6: Assigning the company code to the field status variant in the IMG

As you might have inferred, this is a painstaking and complicated process, especially if you are not an SAP power user or a configuration specialist. As a casual or end user, you would certainly want a much simpler way to customize and personalize your user screen. Let's look at another way to personalize—one that is much more user-friendly.

3.2 Personalization via user parameters

As SAP screens started to become more user-friendly, SAP incorporated the approach of allowing you to save values in fields in SAP transactions to your user profile. This method is called *parameter ID* or *PID*. To enable PID, SAP provides memory variables for some of the most commonly used SAP fields; you assign a particular value to a PID and this information is saved along with your user ID. The next time you access this field, the value that you previously saved in the field is displayed automatically (defaulted). This means that you do not have to memorize the values or search for them. It is an easy way to personalize although it may not be the most convenient one.

Personalization of purchase orders

 Let's illustrate this with a business process that we will be using later for our SAP Fiori proof of concept—creating a purchase order. Assume that you are a procurement officer in your company and the (only) purchasing organization that you are authorized to create orders for is purchasing organization 1000. Therefore, you would like this value to be the default each time you access the purchase order creation screen.

Let's run the purchase order creation transaction (ME21N) and navigate to the ORG. DATA tab. This is shown in Figure 3.7.

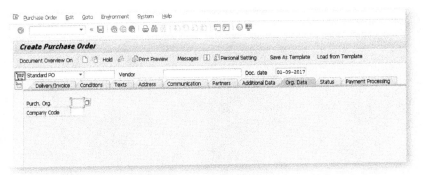

Figure 3.7: Purchase order creation screen

With your cursor on the PURCH. ORG. input field, press F1 on your keyboard and then click the tools icon on the PERFORMANCE ASSISTANT screen as shown in Figure 3.8.

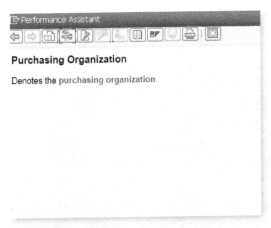

Figure 3.8: Technical information about the purchasing organization field

When you click the tools icon, a number of technical parameters are displayed. The one that is relevant is the field PARAMETER ID and the value **EKO**. This is shown in Figure 3.9.

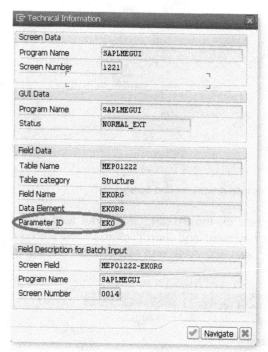

Figure 3.9: Parameter ID information in the technical help

Now enter transaction SU3 (MAINTAIN USER PROFILE) and click the PARAMETERS tab shown in Figure 3.10. Enter the PID for the purchasing organization (**EKO**), type in the value of the purchasing organization you belong to (i.e., **1000**) in the PARAMETER VALUE column, and then save this information.

What was the net outcome of these steps? **1000** is now your default purchasing organization. And in whatever transaction you reference the purchasing organization field, the value of **1000** will be defaulted because it is now tied to your user profile. To confirm this, run the PO creation transaction again. This is shown in Figure 3.11.

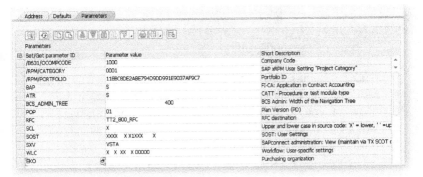

Figure 3.10: Saving the parameter ID value for the purchasing organization in user maintenance

Figure 3.11: PO creation screen with the default purchasing organization value

As you can see in Figure 3.11, the value of **1000** is defaulted in the PURCH. ORG. field.

3.3 Personalization and GuiXT

In the late 1990s, a new SAP personalization product called GuiXT, developed by Synactive Inc., entered the marketplace and first integrated with SAP R/3 version 3.0. GuiXT was designed to work in tandem with SAP's user interface in those days, the SAP GUI. The GuiXT approach is to eliminate the use of ABAP code for customizing and personalizing your SAP user interface.

As SAP's user interface offerings have expanded, so have those of GuiXT. Today it has solutions for mobility, Web UI, offline mode, etc.

GuiXT provides SAP users with a non-disruptive way of reducing the number of fields in an SAP transaction by allowing you to customize SAP screen and business logic via script files. With GuiXT, users can minimize redundant effort (such as using the tab key to bypass fields that have no relevance to your organization) and thereby increase productivity. GuiXT helps you customize your standard SAP transactions to meet a user's specific needs. For example, if a particular user in your organization is only interested in a certain number of fields and only has a limited number of fields he interacts with, GuiXT allows you to hide the redundant fields. If the user wants to change the size and placing of individual fields or wants to add a specific logo to a screen, GuiXT has traditionally been the most effective option.

GuiXT is incorporated into the SAP GUI and is very easy to use. Let us assume you want to use GuiXT for the sales order creation transaction. Either enter transaction code VA01 or navigate in the SAP Easy Access menu as follows (shown in Figure 3.12): LOGISTICS • SALES AND DISTRIBUTION • SALES • ORDER • CREATE.

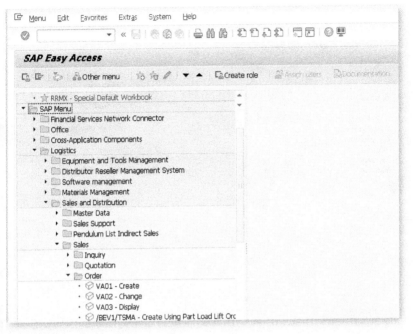

Figure 3.12: Menu path for the sales order creation transaction

Once you have displayed the sales order creation screen, click the 🖳 button at the extreme right and from the drop-down menu, select ACTIVATE GUIXT. This is shown in Figure 3.13.

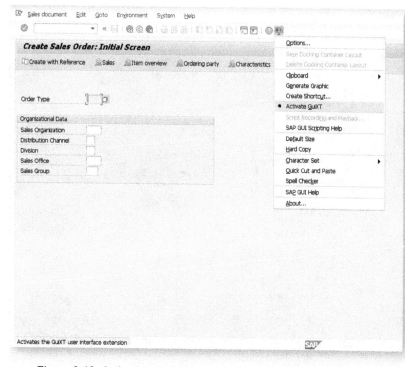

Figure 3.13: Activating GuiXT in the sales order creation transaction

Once you have activated GuiXT for this transaction, a notification message appears indicating that GuiXT has been activated. The SYNACTIVE GUIXT window also appears—this is our entry point for personalization using this tool. The window is shown in Figure 3.14.

From this window, you can perform multiple activities: you can create scripts that control the appearance of a particular screen; you can record your key strokes for a particular screen, etc. A more detailed treatment of GuiXT is beyond the scope of this book. More detailed information is available from the official GuiXT documentation site at *https://www.guixt.com/guixt/*.

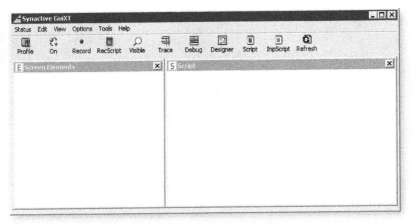

Figure 3.14: GuiXT toolset

In this chapter, I have explained some of the most popular methods for personalizing and customizing your SAP user interfaces to enable a satisfying end user experience. Although these methods are all still very much in use, none of them is a feasible alternative for the regular user. Moreover, they are considerably restrictive and do not work seamlessly across all media. Therefore, the need for a more versatile user experience becomes all the more apparent, and this is what SAP Fiori provides.

I will therefore introduce the concept of SAP Fiori in Chapter 4.

4 SAP Fiori: An overview

A question that many of my customers ask is, "What is SAP Fiori all about?" It's a question that has a significantly long answer because SAP Fiori is not just one thing but rather a convergence of many things. Quite simply, it is SAP's truly new user experience, or for those of you with a technical mindset, it is SAP's new user interface. SAP Fiori marks the end of the era of the traditional gray screens of the flagship SAP GUI, which has existed for over two decades. SAP GUI has been a constant scourge for SAP users worldwide because of the over-abundance of fields and tabs that users have to either enter data in or click through and because of its distinct lack of visual appeal. For those of you interested in statistics, there are over 300,000 individual SAP screens that form the conduit for transactional processing. This is not a trivial number and what bewilders SAP users even today, is that a lot of these screens contain fields that are rarely used and every basic transaction has multiple screens that a user may have to scroll through.

SAP Fiori provides users with a standardized (tile-based) look and feel that is intuitive, visual, and offers fields that are displayed based on the user's roles and authorizations.

At the heart of SAP Fiori is the increasing number of out-of-the-box apps (applications) that SAP provides which correspond to the whole gamut of standard business processes such as order entry (purchase or sales), leave request approval, etc. Currently, there are almost 500 apps available free of charge and if the investment into SAP Fiori is any indication, this number will continue to increase. If the SAP infrastructure prerequisites are met (I will discuss these later), you should be able to be up and running with any such app in a matter of a few hours. When I started my own SAP Fiori odyssey a couple of years ago, it took me approximately six hours to get a standard cost center app up and running. **Disclaimer**: All configuration on the infrastructure side had already been performed by the Basis/NetWeaver administrator and I was able to draw heavily on my years of SAP experience.

SAP Fiori represents a shift from transaction code-based interaction to interaction that is driven by business processes and the users' roles and responsibilities in an organization and as maintained in the SAP security framework. The interaction is heavily influenced by the seismic shift that has taken place in the consumer marketplace, where business is increasingly transacted on mobile devices via simple apps. SAP Fiori leverages this concept to provide the same end user experience that eschews exposing the complexity of the solution and provides users with an engaging experience. It is based on the theory of "build once, run everywhere". Therefore, with SAP Fiori, your app will run on your desktop as well as your mobile device and will look and feel exactly the same on both: you do not have to create a separate desktop version of your app and a separate one for your mobile device.

As the years have gone by, SAP's advertising campaigns bear testimony to how the focus has shifted from highlighting its all-encompassing and integrated nature to a simplified, user-driven software suite. The journey from *The Best Run Businesses Run SAP* to *Run Simple* has seen SAP go through many ups and downs and detours, including multiple acquisitions and strategy changes, as it has evolved from an introverted German software maker to a global innovation factory that provides speedy solutions with a high business ROI. And one of the primary lessons that SAP has learned well is that no matter how wonderfully efficient the software engineering is, it is ultimately the user experience that counts.

SAP Fiori apps have been designed using certain platform-agnostic design tools such as HTML5, JavaScript, and CSS. This combination of tools has been wrapped into something called SAP UI5 but I will come back to this a little later. As a result, SAP Fiori apps can be rendered on all kinds of mobile devices without the need for any software magic such as creating wrappers to ensure compatibility. Furthermore, this framework also provides users with a convenient means to enhance existing apps and incorporate users' business needs.

SAP Fiori and NetWeaver security

 A question that is often asked is whether SAP Fiori leverages the SAP NetWeaver security framework or whether you have to design security separately for SAP Fiori. The good news is that SAP Fiori allows you to leverage your existing NetWeaver security model. In fact, when you configure any app, the visibility and access are determined by the roles and authorizations that particular user is assigned to.

4.1 Why SAP Fiori?

This is a question that you will be asked frequently (if you haven't already been asked). As SAP expands SAP Fiori both horizontally and vertically, more and more companies will want to implement SAP Fiori in some shape or form. You will therefore need to be ready to answer this question in a precise manner. If you are trying to "sell" SAP Fiori within your organization, you should emphasize the following:

▶ **Vastly enhanced end user experience**: This aspect of SAP Fiori stands out immediately. Whether it is on your desktop/laptop or on your mobile device (e.g., an iPad), starting with the SAP Fiori launchpad you see a vastly improved and user-friendly user interface that almost seems to beg the question, "Is this really an SAP product"? This has frequently been my own experience, especially with an audience that is quite acclimatized to the other types of SAP user interfaces.

▶ **Rapidly increasing out-of-the box inventory**: It is hard to keep track of the volume of SAP Fiori apps that SAP keeps releasing. What makes it non-disruptive is that these apps work on your back-end SAP transactions and business processes. There is no need to redesign or change anything in your transactional processing. SAP Fiori seamlessly leverages these business processes.

▶ **Role-based approach**: SAP Fiori apps address business processes, business needs, and roles. Therefore, access to these apps and the functionality that they encapsulate is based on the roles and profiles that a user has in the system. These roles have already been set up in the system and SAP Fiori leverages these existing roles.

- ► **Single development paradigm for multiple devices**: You cannot stress this point enough. With SAP Fiori, there is no longer any need to question how your application will be rendered on SAP GUI versus Web GUI versus Web Dynpro and so on. You only develop once and the application has the same look and feel regardless of the device it is deployed on.

- ► **Limitless opportunities to customize**: Due to the complexities involved in customizing standard SAP screens, customers had to grudgingly accept what they got. Consequently, they had to go through multiple screens and countless fields to complete even the simplest of transactions. SAP Fiori is much more user-friendly in this regard.

4.2   Cost of SAP Fiori

When SAP Fiori was first introduced by SAP and up until the Sapphire/ASUG Annual Conference of 2014, customers had to pay for SAP Fiori licenses separately. The cost of each individual user license was approximately $150 plus additional licensing costs. If you were looking to roll out SAP Fiori across a significantly large user base (say 5000 users, for example), you would potentially have been looking at a pretty hefty investment. The cost of an SAP Fiori license became a matter of much debate and angst among the SAP user community, to put it mildly. Users are surely correct in expecting an intuitive, pleasant, and friendly user interface free of charge. So is it justifiable to charge for the kind of user interface and experience that SAP users should have been provided with many years ago? And will companies be willing to pay for more than a few licenses, if any? A pleasant user experience, if not necessarily a memorable one, is something users expect as a bare minimum from every application. In this day and age of app-driven user interfaces that require very little imagination, training, and effort to be productive, it is reasonable for the average user to expect a user interface that is simple yet engaging and most importantly, to not have to pay any premium for it. Fortunately, SAP has heard the resounding message from customers worldwide about the long overdue need for a better user experience at no extra price. Therefore, the TCO of SAP Fiori does not entail any license costs. It is entirely made up of the labor/contract costs for installing, implementing, and configuring SAP Fiori and any other infrastructure costs.

So what does this all mean? If you are an existing SAP customer, with effect from June 2014, SAP Fiori is available to you at no additional cost. It is bundled into your existing license and maintenance agreements with SAP. And what if you were charged a license fee for SAP Fiori prior to June 2014? In this case, SAP will provide you with a credit.

SAP Fiori cost disclaimer

 The disclaimer I would like to include here is that licensing is a very customer-specific area. Standard licensing agreements are like the manufacturer's suggested retail price (MSRP) for automobiles that are sold by dealerships in the US. As a customer, you rarely end up paying the MSRP depending on how well you have bargained and this itself could be influenced by your relationship with the dealer. Therefore, with regard to licensing, you should confer with your SAP Account Executive.

4.3   The waves of SAP Fiori

To complement the artistic ambitions of SAP Fiori, SAP has been releasing apps in *waves* instead of in support packages or enhancement packages. The waves are as follows:

▶ **Wave 1**: In this first wave, which was released in May 2013, 25 transactional apps covering certain ECC and SRM business processes were released. Because this was the first "release" of SAP Fiori, the different categories for SAP Fiori apps had not yet been established. Some of the apps that customers implemented in this wave were approval/workflow type apps, such as leave requests, travel requests, purchase orders, requisitions, etc., or standard business processes, such as create/change sales orders, etc.

▶ **Wave 2:** In this second release (November 2013), SAP significantly expanded the range of apps offered to cover business processes in ECC, SRM, CRM, GRC, etc. The wave contained the following:
   – 28 new transactional apps
   – 69 (new) fact sheets
   – 83 analytical apps

   With the release of Wave 2, the total number of SAP Fiori apps available for usage reached almost 200. Also, with Wave 2, the SAP Fiori apps were categorized as transactional apps, analytical apps, and fact sheets.

▶ **Wave 3:** This minor release, made available in February 2014, added 8 new transactional apps and 2 new analytical apps.

▶ **Wave 4:** With this release in May 2014, to generally coincide with the Sapphire/ASUG 2014 Annual Conference, SAP made its intentions regarding SAP Fiori clear: it added over 100 new apps, including 24 new transactional apps, 7 new fact sheets, and 58 new analytical apps, bringing the total number of apps available to around 320. It is important to note that owing to the strong customer demand for a better end user experience at no additional cost, SAP decided to provide these apps free of charge to companies that had already paid for certain types of licenses (to be discussed later).

▶ **Wave 5:** On the heels of Wave 4 came Wave 5 in July 2014, with 32 new transactional apps, 5 new fact sheets, and 21 new analytical apps, taking the total number of SAP Fiori apps to almost 380.

▶ **Wave 6:** In October 2014, Wave 6 was released. The SAP Fiori arsenal was significantly expanded with almost 100 new apps, including 40 new transactional apps, 13 new fact sheets, and almost 50 new analytical apps.

▶ **Wave 7:** Released in early 2015, this wave expanded the SAP Fiori arsenal even further, with the total number of apps crossing the 500 mark.

New apps will continue to be released bundled in new waves. The best source of information on new releases/waves/apps is the SAP Help website. You can access the SAP Fiori area at: *https://help.sap.com/fiori*.

4.4 SAP Fiori 2.0

With effect from October 2015, there is a new kid on the block: SAP Fiori 2.0 represents a revamped look for SAP Fiori. The need for a more streamlined and appealing design was largely driven by the exploding portfolio of SAP Fiori apps. What is more, the navigational habits of users are considerably different with such a large number of apps compared to the first couple of SAP Fiori waves (when there were only a couple of hundred apps). Some of the apps interact with one another. And from October 2016, 2.0 is packaged with S/4HANA 1610. How does 2.0 differ from the 1.0 series of apps? The following is a brief list of some of the differences:

- ▶ The somewhat plain look of the launchpad has been enhanced with some new features that make personalization easier
- ▶ Improved overall placement of functions
- ▶ Better navigation
- ▶ The (ubiquitous) Blue Crystal design that has been the background (or theme in SAP parlance) for all of SAP Fiori 1.0 has been replaced with the Belize design. This new design enables better navigation and a better end user experience overall

Figure 4.1 and Figure 4.2 show the screens in SAP Fiori 2.0.

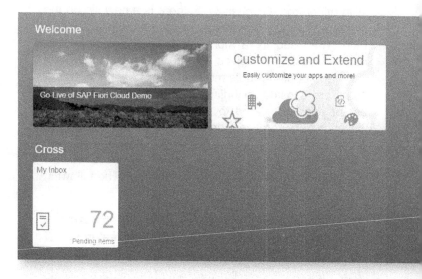

Figure 4.1: SAP Fiori launchpad in Version 2.0

Figure 4.2: Sample PO details in SAP Fiori 2.0

In the next chapter, we will look more closely at the technical aspects of SAP Fiori.

5 SAP Fiori: A technical deep dive

So far, I have taken you through the evolution of user interfaces and the associated technologies and also introduced to you the concept of SAP Fiori from a high level. It is now time to dive deep into the technical aspects of SAP Fiori. Let us start by looking at the various categories of SAP Fiori apps.

5.1 Categories of SAP Fiori apps

Currently, there are three categories of SAP Fiori apps:

1. Transactional apps

As the name suggests, these are apps that allow you to execute business transactions. Typical examples of such apps are creating/changing purchase/sales orders, creating invoices, releasing production orders, etc. This is the most popular category of apps because these apps correspond to key business processes that any business will typically run. Although SAP is putting all its energies into trying to take HANA mainstream, this category of apps does not require a HANA database. In my discussions with a lot of existing and prospective customers, this seems to be a key determining factor because a lot of SAP customers have not implemented HANA and are not planning to do so in the immediate future.

SAP HANA

 HANA is an acronym for High-performance Analytic Appliance and it is SAP's comprehensive platform that allows complex and high-volume transactions and analytics to be processed extremely quickly and stored in the HANA in-memory columnar database. First released in late 2011, HANA has become SAP's platform for the future. More detailed information about SAP HANA can be found at *http://www.sap.com/product/technology-platform/hana.html*. I cover a relevant component of SAP HANA, SAP S/4HANA, in Section 5.5 of this book.

Figure 5.1 shows the building blocks of transactional apps.

Let us now try and understand how an SAP Fiori transactional app works and what the prerequisites and components are. You will need SAP Business Suite running on top of your database (as I just mentioned, this could be any database, including SAP HANA). At the heart of this architecture is SAP NetWeaver Gateway, which resides in your ABAP front-end server. This is part of your SAP NetWeaver technical stack and is the conduit that enables multiple SAP Business Suite systems (such as ECC, SCM, CRM, etc.) to interact with the client (i.e., mobile device, desktop, etc.) through something called OData. We will look at OData in more detail in Section 5.5.

You do not have to use the Gateway server—this is the case, for example, when you are connecting to a single ERP or SRM system.

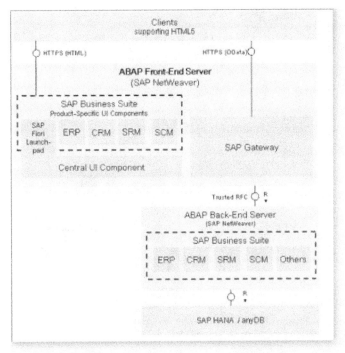

Figure 5.1: Technical architecture of transactional apps (source: SAP)

2. Analytical apps

Analytical apps complement your transactional apps by enabling you to view numerical information (such as amounts and quantities). These apps are less common than their transactional counterparts, probably owing to the fact that they need a HANA database to run on. These apps could almost be considered as dashboards that display the most important key performance indicators (KPIs) for your business. Figure 5.2 shows the overall technical framework that underpins SAP Fiori analytical apps.

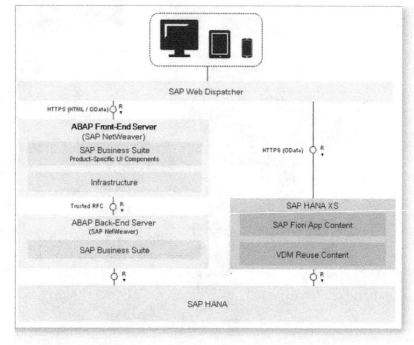

Figure 5.2: Technical architecture of analytical apps (source: SAP)

3. Fact sheets

Fact sheets add value to your transactional and analytical apps by providing you with additional information on the key objects in your transactional and analytical apps. You can also add a fact sheet to an existing fact sheet. The best way to understand the functionality of a fact sheet is to think of a typical invoice: a fact sheet allows you to drill down into the line items of this invoice. At the time of writing, fact sheets run only on a HANA database. Figure 5.3 shows the technical architecture of fact sheets.

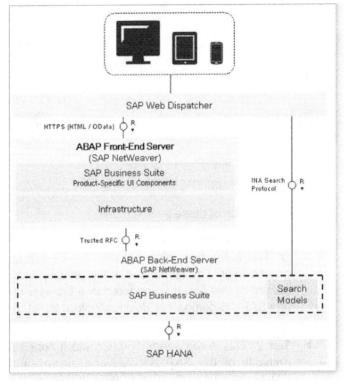

Figure 5.3: Technical architecture of fact sheets (source: SAP)

5.2 SAP Fiori architecture

Let us now look more closely at the architecture of SAP Fiori and try to deconstruct the various pieces. The SAP Fiori stack consists of three tiers, as shown in Figure 5.4.

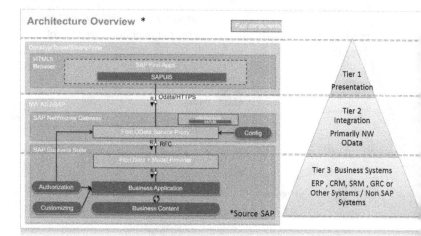

Figure 5.4: SAP Fiori technical stack

Let us look at each of these tiers in detail.

▶ Tier 1: You can consider this the *presentation* tier. This is the tier which you will interact with as an end user. The launchpad is the primary component of this tier. It is rendered in a browser on any SAPUI5-compatible desktop/laptop, tablet, or smartphone.

▶ Tier 2: This is the *integration* tier and it consists primarily of the SAP NetWeaver Gateway and OData services. It is the glue between the presentation tier and the back-end (i.e., tier 3).

▶ Tier 3: This is the *data* tier and it consists of one or more systems in which data reside. Data for SAP Fiori could be provided by SAP ERP, CRM, SRM, or even non-SAP systems.

SAP Fiori with NetWeaver

 A lot of organizations find the most compelling use cases for SAP Fiori in their ERP transaction system. Most commonly, it happens to be an ECC 6.0 system. The minimum requirement on the back-end is Support Package stack (SPS) 15.

In the middle tier, it is very common to have SAP NetWeaver Gateway. Because this component is embedded in SAP NetWeaver, your Basis administrator will have to configure the settings to enable it for SAP Fiori.

5.3 Prerequisites for SAP Fiori

If you want to configure/run an SAP Fiori app on your SAP ECC system, there are a few technical prerequisites that must be satisfied. These are as follows:

- ▶ SAP ERP 6.0 SPS 15 or higher
- ▶ SAP ERP 6.0 EhP2 SPS 06 or higher
- ▶ SAP ERP 6.0 EhP3 SPS 05 or higher
- ▶ SAP ERP 6.0 EhP4 SPS 05 or higher
- ▶ SAP ERP 6.0 EhP5 SPS 03 or higher
- ▶ SAP ERP 6.0 EhP6 SPS 01 or higher
- ▶ SAP NetWeaver Gateway 2.0 SPS 07
- ▶ SAP NetWeaver 7.0 SPS 21 or higher

It might be obvious to you but it is still worth stating that if you are on an ECC release that is below 6.0, you will have to upgrade to at least ECC 6.0 SPS 15 to be able to meet the basic prerequisites for SAP Fiori. Some organizations are using this as a rationale for upgrading from ECC 5.0 or lower to ECC 6.0.

5.4 Key technical components of SAP Fiori

There are a couple of technologies and technical terms in the SAP Fiori realm that do not belong to the conventional SAP world. Let's go through the key ones since you will encounter them frequently:

▶ **OData:** This stands for *Open Data*, a protocol which, according to Wikipedia, "allows the creation and consumption of queryable and interoperable RESTful APIs in a simple and standard way" (*https://en.wikipedia.org/wiki/Open_Data_Protocol*). It is a mystery to me why it was abbreviated to OData (when Open Data would have been perfectly acceptable) but we will let someone else solve that one. The OData protocol was introduced by Microsoft. So why is OData important for SAP Fiori? The answer is because SAP wanted SAP Fiori to be a web-based user interface that abstracts the user experience (whether through laptops or mobile devices) from the complexity of the transaction system (usually an ERP, BW, or CRM system). OData allows Web clients to publish and edit resources—identified using URLs and defined in a data model—using simple HTTP messages via production and consumption of REST APIs. Stripping all the geek-speak out, using the OData protocol helps SAP adhere to open standards. And the benefits to SAP of adhering to open standards are that it helps developers build applications in a variety of different technologies and the functionality that is thus created works across all devices.

▶ **REST:** This is another acronym that is extremely popular these days because it is becoming a global standard; it stands for *representational state transfer*, which is a specific type of web service. Again, I am leaning on Wikipedia to provide the most succinct definition of REST: "REST-compliant web services allow requesting systems to access and manipulate textual representations of web resources using a uniform and predefined set of stateless operation." (*https://en.wikipedia. org/wiki/Representational_state_transfer*). And why is REST important for you? For many reasons: this protocol strives for better performance between the sender and the receiver, greater reliability of the data that is shared, portability of code and data, a simple and intuitive user interface, and the ability to scale as the number of components and the number of interactions among them increases.

▶ **SAP NetWeaver Gateway:** This is a conventional SAP term. It is basically a framework that allows SAP systems to connect to other systems and devices using open standards and protocols. It helps SAP leverage non-native standards and technologies using *Application Programming Interfaces (APIs)* and protocols and services such as REST and OData.

▶ **SAP UI 5:** This is also known as *SAP User Interface for HTML5*. Technically speaking, it is SAP's version of HTML5 and is a comprehensive client-side development framework that enables developers to design device-agnostic user interfaces that can meet their highest aesthetic standards. SAP UI 5 has two other technical pillars called CSS and JavaScript. Again, why is this important for you? The reason is that all SAP Fiori apps have been designed using SAP UI 5 and in order to create new apps and/or modify/extend existing apps, your development team will need to have expertise in SAP UI 5. While you can view SAP UI 5 as proprietary to SAP, there is an Open Source version of it called *OpenUI5 of GitHub*. Strategically speaking, SAP UI 5 represents SAP's response to the ever-changing needs of user interfaces given the multitude of device types available today. With this technology, SAP can deliver a consistent user experience across any device as well as achieve the separation between the business transaction and the user interaction.

5.5   SAP Fiori and S/4HANA

SAP Fiori and S/4HANA are intricately connected. It is therefore worth digressing slightly to understand what S/4HANA is all about. S/4HANA is the completely revamped application software suite that succeeds the R/3 generation. It is built on the robust foundation that HANA provides and therefore S/4 fully leverages HANA's in-memory capabilities. By significantly simplifying the software design, S/4 now has a much more streamlined design with fewer tables (and thus a much smaller memory footprint), application simplification, and better application performance. When SAP Fiori was first designed and released, it was conceived as SAP's next generation user interface. At that time, however, S/4 was still on the drawing board. As SAP accelerated its S/4 momentum and embarked on an almost complete makeover of its application suite, it naturally determined SAP Fiori to be the cornerstone of its simplified and enhanced user experience. Today, SAP Fiori has become an almost inextricable part of S/4.

The S/4 suite comes in two flavors: the *on-premise* edition and the *cloud* option. When S/4HANA is installed on-premise, the SAP Fiori installation is included. When you subscribe to the cloud edition, no installation is necessary. SAP Fiori is part of the end user interface and it comes pre-packaged with multiple business scenarios.

When SAP released its S/4HANA 1610 on-premise version in October 2016 and 1611 cloud version in November 2016, it provided multiple SAP Fiori apps that you can use right out of the box.

I have encountered a lot of confusion and many misperceptions regarding the relationship between SAP Fiori and S/4HANA. I will therefore attempt to clarify these. Here are a few important things you should be aware of:

▶ You can use SAP Fiori for certain SAP business processes. You should not expect to interact with the SAP back-end for all transaction codes in S/4 in the on-premise version.

▶ It is highly unlikely that SAP will enable every single standard transaction code for SAP Fiori. One reason for this could be that there is really no need to do so because it could result in redundancies.

▶ SAP S/4HANA cloud edition exclusively leverages SAP Fiori screens. You might wonder why this is the case—it is because the cloud edition supports a vastly reduced set of standard business processes.

▶ In the latest release of S/4HANA releases a lot of the SAP business processes across multiple modules leverage SAP Fiori 2.0. In fact, the use of SAP Fiori 2.0 has been made mandatory starting with this release. What this means is that the only way to access an app in this release is by using SAP Fiori 2.0. The next (on-premise) version is likely to extend SAP Fiori to even more business processes.

In this chapter I addressed the technical aspect of SAP Fiori and also explored the relationship between SAP Fiori and HANA. You should now have a sufficiently strong understanding of the technical underpinnings of SAP Fiori. We are now ready to go to a level deeper and look at installing and configuring SAP Fiori in your environment.

6 Installing and configuring SAP Fiori

We are now ready to proceed deeper into technical SAP Fiori territory. You might recall reading earlier that a lot of effort has to be invested upfront before you can deploy your first SAP Fiori app. The key thing to remember is that whether you are deploying one app or multiple apps, the basic installation steps are the same. A large proportion of the configuration is also the same and is not dependent on the number of apps you plan to roll out. However, when you arrive at the level of deploying individual apps, you will very probably have to perform some app-specific customization. Let us start with the installation of SAP Fiori.

6.1 SAP Fiori deployment options

Before you proceed with your installation, you will need to make an important architectural decision—that is, what your installation model is going to be. Currently, there are two popular deployment options for SAP NetWeaver Gateway:

▶ **Option 1a: Central hub deployment (with everything on one server):** In this option, all the SAP NetWeaver Gateway-related services are deployed on one server. This server is therefore designated as the central hub. The key characteristic of this option is that there is no development or configuration required on the back-end ECC system. While that might seem like a good separation of duties, the constraint that this approach imposes is that there is no direct access channel between the hub and the data in the connected ECC system. You are restricted to using the existing communication conduits such as *Remote Function Calls (RFCs)* and *Business Application Programming Interfaces (BAPIs)* to exchange information with your back-end SAP systems. One of the biggest advantages is that you have a centralized means of accessing the back-end system.

▶ **Option 1b: Central hub deployment (with development in the back-end system):** In this option, the SAP NetWeaver Gateway software (along with the front-end services and other runtime services) is installed on the SAP NetWeaver Gateway (hub) server. Configuration and development takes place in the connected back-end (ECC) system.

If you are not a Basis administrator or an SAP technical expert, the best way to understand central hub deployment is to look at it as a single home for both your front-end and back-end services.

▶ **Option 2: Embedded deployment:** This is the "all-in-one" model. All Gateway, front-end, and back-end services are bundled and deployed in one system. That system is typically your ERP/ECC back-end system. Although it might seem convenient to deploy everything on one system, do consider the additional processing burden that the system will have to bear if you plan on introducing other systems into the mix and your "all-in-one" system has to start acting as a hub.

6.2 Installing SAP Fiori

Installing SAP Fiori involves multiple components. Because most of these steps are highly technical in nature, I will not dwell on them too much. In most cases, I will simply provide you with the necessary pointers.

The six essential steps are as follows:

1. **Install the back-end components on your SAP ERP environment(s).** Prior to doing this, check whether your SAP NetWeaver system satisfies the SAP Fiori prerequisites. This information is available from any standard SAP screen by navigating as follows: SYSTEM • STATUS • COMPONENT INFORMATION. A screen like the one shown in Figure 6.1 appears.

Figure 6.1: Information on the SAP software installed in your SAP system

Click the INSTALLED PRODUCT VERSIONS tab to access further valuable information. This is shown in Figure 6.2.

Product	Release	Vendor	Short Description of Product Version
SAP PPIM	5.0	sap.com	SAP PORTF AND PROJ MGMT 5.0
SAP CORE CEE	110_604	sap.com	SAP CORE CEE 110_604
SAP HR-CEE	110_604	sap.com	SAP HR-CEE 110_604
SAP REACH COMPLIANCE	2.0	sap.com	SAP REACH COMPLIANCE 2.0
SAP GRC ACCESS CONTROL	600	sap.com	SAP ACCESS CONTROL 10.0
SAP GRC PROCESS CONTROL	600	sap.com	SAP PROCESS CONTROL 10.0
SAP GRC GLOBAL TRADE SERVICES	SAP GTS 9.0	sap.com	SAP GTS 10.0
QAM	1.0	sap.com	SAP QUALITY ISSUE MGMT 1.0
BOBJDQFS	4.0	sap.com	SBOP DQM FOR SAP SOL. 4.0
SUPPLY_MARKET_COLLABORATION	100	sap.com	SAP SUPPL. LIFECYCLE MGMT. 1.0
SAP ENTERPR PROJ CONN	200_600	sap.com	SAP ENTERPR PROJ CONN 2.0 60
SAP EHS MGMT. EXTENSION	3.0	sap.com	SAP EHS MGMT. EXTENSION 3.0
SAP MANAGEMENT OF CHANGE	1.0	sap.com	SAP MANAGEMENT OF CHANGE 1.0
SAP WS&O BY CLICKSOFTWARE	2.1.6	sap.com	SAP WS&O BY CLICKSOFTWARE2.1.6
EHP7 FOR SAP ERP 6.0	EHP7 FOR SAP ERP 6.0	sap.com	EHP7 FOR SAP ERP 6.0
SAP WORKFORCE DEPLOYMENT	1.0	sap.com	SAP WORKFORCE DEPLOYMENT 1.0
SAP ERP	2005	sap.com	SAP ERP 6.0

Figure 6.2: Information on the product versions installed in your SAP system

2. **Install SAP NetWeaver Gateway.** In order to do this, you will need to download the SAP NetWeaver Gateway components from the SAP software download site at *https://service.sap.com/swdc*. Please note that in order to do so, you will need a valid user and password. This is also assuming that your company has bought the relevant SAP licenses for you to be eligible for downloads. The next four steps are part of the installation procedure. I will not go into the details because these activities will be performed by your SAP NetWeaver administrator.

3. Install SAP UI components

4. Install SAP Web Dispatcher

5. Install SAP Enterprise Portal

6. Install SAP Mobile Platform

6.3 Configuring SAP Fiori (Gateway activities)

Once SAP Fiori has been installed in your environment, there are many configuration activities that will have to be performed. As a (business) user, these may not be of much interest to you. However, if you are a developer or a NetWeaver/Basis administrator, or are interested in the technical aspects of SAP Fiori, they will certainly interest you.

Installation guide for SAP Fiori

Note that the source for these activities is the installation guide for SAP Fiori and I am presenting it here in condensed form with appropriate commentary.

Activity 1: Activate services in the SAP NetWeaver Gateway system

In this activity, you activate a number of services in transaction SICF.

Activity 2: Create connections between the hub system and source SAP systems

For each source SAP system that will be passing through the SAP NetWeaver Gateway hub, you will need to create a trusted RFC connection. This step is not necessary for the local deployment option. The step also involves creating an RFC on SAP NetWeaver Gateway to the connected SAP system and defining a trusted connection between SAP NetWeaver Gateway and the connected SAP system.

Activity 3: Create the SAP system alias for applications

The configuration setting for this activity can be performed by navigating in the IMG as follows (shown in Figure 6.3): SAP NETWEAVER • GATEWAY • ODATA CHANNEL • CONFIGURATION • CONNECTION SETTINGS • SAP NETWEAVER GATEWAY TO SAP SYSTEM • MANAGE SAP SYSTEM ALIASES.

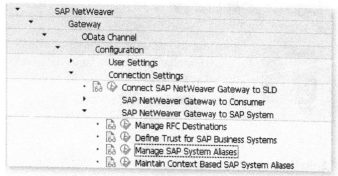

Figure 6.3: Managing SAP system aliases in the IMG

Activity 4: Check the SAP system aliases

There are a few activities that you will have to perform in this step in your SAP NetWeaver Gateway system. The transaction code for this activity is IWFND/CHECK_ALIASES. All of these steps involve checking whether the connections you have set up in the previous systems are correct or not. The activities involve checking the status (red, green, or yellow) of the connections.

Activity 5: Activate SAP NetWeaver Gateway

Once you have performed all the preceding steps, you are ready to activate SAP NetWeaver Gateway. Figure 6.4 shows the relevant menu: SAP NETWEAVER • GATEWAY • ODATA CHANNEL • CONFIGURATION • ACTIVATE OR DEACTIVATE SAP NETWEAVER GATEWAY.

Figure 6.4: Activating SAP NetWeaver Gateway in the IMG

Activity 6: Add and activate the SAP NetWeaver Gateway and UI5 services

As the name suggests, in this activity, you activate and maintain the relevant services. Your NetWeaver adminstrator will know what services to activate and maintain so I will not show you the entire list. It is sufficient to know the menu path. This is shown in Figure 6.5: SAP NETWEAVER • GATEWAY • ODATA CHANNEL • ADMINISTRATION • GENERAL SETTINGS • ACTIVATE AND MAINTAIN SERVICES.

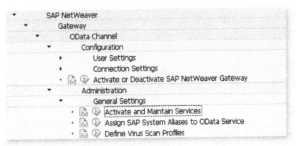

Figure 6.5: Activating and maintaining services in the IMG

6.4 Configuring SAP Fiori (launchpad activities)

You have now completed the back-end configuration activities and are ready to configure your SAP Fiori launchpad, also commonly referred to as the front-end configuration. In order to create a new launchpad, you have to perform a set of configuration steps in your source ECC system. Please note that all these activities will be (or at least should be) executed by your NetWeaver administrator. Therefore, I will not walk you through all the steps involved. It is highly likely that you will not have to do anything here because a standard SAP Fiori app will already have been fully configured for you.

Configuration activities

You will only have to perform these configuration activities if you need to create a new launchpad or, more correctly, a new view of the launchpad.

Step 1: The first step is to run transaction LPD_CUST to access the launchpad maintenance screen as shown in Figure 6.6.

Step 2: You create a new launchpad by clicking NEW LAUNCHPAD. A dialog box appears where you have to enter the necessary parameters to start on this process. Figure 6.7 shows this dialog box. As a minimum, you should enter values for the mandatory fields (ROLE, IN-STANCE, and DESCRIPTION).

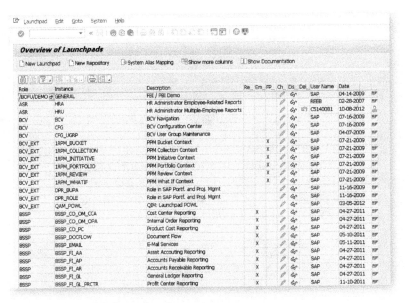

Figure 6.6: Launchpad overview

Figure 6.7: Creating a new launchpad

Step 3: You now have to create a new application corresponding to the new launchpad by clicking the NEW APPLICATION button shown in Figure 6.8. The panel on the right-hand side of the screen contains a few fields in which you have to enter information, including the LINK TEXT and the APPLICATION TYPE fields.

Figure 6.8: Creating a new application for the Launchpad

We want the application type to be URL and when we choose **URL** from the drop-down list, an additional button SHOW ADVANCED (OPTIONAL) PARAMETERS appears. This is shown in Figure 6.9. Note that if you choose the **URL** option, you will need to provide the URL.

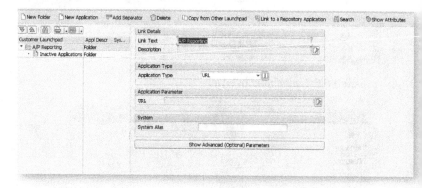

Figure 6.9: Advanced optional parameters when creating a new application

When you press the SHOW ADVANCED (OPTIONAL) PA-RAMETERS button, a number of optional fields are displayed. All you need to know is that these will control one or more aspects of your interaction with the app on the launchpad.

Step 4: You now create a tile for your SAP Fiori launchpad. In order to do so, you have to map the target in the launchpad designer. Here, you specify the relevant parameters that will bind your tile to the application.

These parameters include the role, ID, etc. You can also customize this tile to display a logo and text of your choice.

Step 5: The final step in this process is to map the launchpad role to the corresponding catalog. A catalog is a collection of apps that is accessible to a specific role. In a classical SAP sense, you can think of it as the menu that you see when you login to your SAP ECC system. You perform this mapping in the SAP role maintenance transaction (PFCG).

In this chapter, I took you deep into the heart of SAP Fiori's technical foundations. We are now ready to move to the next chapter to discuss rapid rollout of SAP Fiori.

7 Rapid implementation of SAP Fiori

The experience of implementing SAP Fiori in your organization does not have to be similar to implementing one or more SAP modules. The latter implementation typically cannot be done quickly and generally goes through a waterfall approach. SAP's conventional methodology for this approach is called ASAP. However, in recent years, it has become possible to implement and deploy a lot of SAP modules and applications quickly primarily by adopting an agile approach. A specific example of this is the increasing availability of SAP *rapid-deployment solutions (RDS)* for its new offerings. When SAP HANA was introduced, SAP launched multiple rapid-deployment solutions to enable faster implementation and acceptance of HANA. SAP has continued in this tradition with SAP Fiori. The move towards faster implementation and deployment has been further enabled by the move to the cloud, which by its very nature dramatically shortens certain time-consuming activities such as hardware procurement, installation, etc.

7.1 SAP Fiori rapid-deployment solutions: Overview

SAP provides various rapid-deployment solution options that enable your company to implement one or more SAP Fiori apps and/or scenarios. But why is this important for you? SAP lists the following positive aspects as factors you should consider:

▶ Fast
▶ Predictable
▶ Seamless
▶ Simple

I would add a couple of other benefits of using this approach to the list:

▶ Risk mitigation: in the world of application software, businesses often take on a high degree of risk when they undertake to build and deploy a complex solution. The magnitude of this risk increases if your business is relatively new to the technology and/or is implementing it for the first time. In this case, I would recommend using a rapid-deployment solution. It will probably be more expensive at face value compared to building and deploying a solution on your own, but it is likely to be cheaper and more effective in the long run.

▶ Best practices: with a rapid-deployment solution deployed by SAP or one of its partners, you will be able to learn from best practices. Not only will you have an opportunity to observe and participate in the project, but you will also learn best practices that the experts have compiled. This will help you to succeed in your subsequent SAP Fiori rollouts.

Rapid-deployment solutions as accelerators

 You should view SAP Fiori rapid-deployment solutions as accelerators that speed up the establishment of rapid-deployment solutions in your organization. The true value that these rapid-deployment solutions provide is in accelerating the pace of SAP Fiori deployment in your organization by giving you access to a wide set of tools and methodologies.

Figure 7.1 shows a partial screenshot of some of the different types of SAP rapid-deployment solutions available to you.

	Fiori Apps RDS	Fiori Infrastructure RDS	SAPUI5 Design RDS	HANA Live RDS
Theme	• Deploy fresh, delightful, and easy to use multi-channel apps on top of the existing business suite for customers not yet using SAP HANA	• Accelerate the adoption of SAP's new user experience for Suite on HANA and enable landscape to be ready for HANA-optimized Fiori apps	• Design and create new Fiori-designed transactional applications based on the SAPUI5 SDK and SAP UI/UX design best practices	• Enables real-time reporting on Business Suite operational data. Provides pre-built reporting content and pre-configured content based on HANA Live virtual data models.
Target Group	• Existing ECC6 customers • IT / Security experts	• New HANA customers • IT / Security experts	• Partners and existing ECC customers • UI / UX developers	• New HANA customers • Existing ECC customers
Application Content	• 25 wave 1 transactional applications • 19 wave 2 transactional applications (including down-ported transactional apps)	• ~180 HANA optimized apps (Analytics, CRM, Sales, Finance, Manufacturing, Factsheets)	• Sample apps demonstrating the main Fiori design types for transactional scenarios	• 10 Smart Business applications • 3 Fiori Analytical applications
Technology	• SAP ERP 6 EhP1 – EhP7 • SAP NW Gateway 7.31 / 7.4 • SAPUI5 V.1	• EhP7 SP2 and other SP • SAP NW 7.4 • HANA DB	• SAP NW Gateway 7.31 / 7.4 • SAPUI5 V.1 • SAPUI5 Fiori extensions	• ERP6.0 SP12, CRM 7.0 SP09 • HANA Live 1.0 • SAP NW 7.4 • HANA DB

Figure 7.1: Extract of some SAP Fiori rapid-deployment solutions

7.2 How do you find the right SAP Fiori rapid-deployment solution?

SAP provides rapid-deployment solutions for each of the three categories of SAP Fiori apps. Information on each of these rapid-deployment solutions is available from the following website: *https://rapid.sap.com/bp/#/RDS_FIORI*. Figure 7.2 shows a partial screenshot of the landing page.

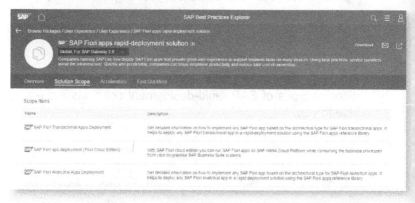

Figure 7.2: Partial view of the SAP Fiori rapid-deployment solution landing page

The overview section introduces the concept of SAP Fiori rapid-deployment solutions, the business benefits, the key competitive differentiators, and the software requirements.

For a summary of each rapid-deployment solution by category, click the SOLUTION SCOPE tab. If you are interested in the fact sheets app deployment rapid-deployment solution, click SAP FIORI FACTSHEET APPS DEPLOYMENT. This takes you to the next information page that will help you to understand the components and capabilities of this rapid-deployment solution.

On the ACCELERATORS tab, you can find information on all the prerequisites for implementing a particular SAP Fiori rapid-deployment solution.

In this chapter, we took a brief look at how you can accelerate the introduction and assimilation of SAP Fiori in your organization by using the rapid-deployment solution approach and where to find rapid-deployment solutions. We are now ready to move to another important component of SAP Fiori—the launchpad.

8 The SAP Fiori launchpad

The SAP Fiori launchpad is your entry point into the world of SAP Fiori. You can think of it as a gateway or portal that gives you access to the apps/applications for which you have authorization. The first ever gateway to SAP Fiori was released commercially in May 2013. It was called SAP Fiori Launch Page. The product we call the launchpad was released at the end of 2013 and was a significant improvement in both form and function over its predecessor.

8.1 Introduction to the SAP Fiori launchpad

As stated above, the launchpad is your gateway to SAP Fiori. It is where your interaction with SAP Fiori will begin. The launchpad serves as a front-end service that renders each user's personalized app portal. It can also be considered as a user's home page for his interaction with various back-end systems.

Launchpad—home of apps

 For those of you interested in the technical aspects, the launchpad is meant to be a medium where apps developed in all kinds of technologies run. The apps that run in the launchpad are housed in containers and although the apps may have been built on various different platforms, such as ABAP, UI5, etc., they are rendered in the same manner in the launchpad across all devices.

8.2 Features of the launchpad

What is so special about this launchpad and why is it important for users? There are many reasons:

▶ All you need to do to start the launchpad is type the relevant URL into any Internet-ready device. Therefore, all you really need to be able to use SAP Fiori (assuming of course that you have the requisite authorizations and authentication) is availability to a device that connects to the Internet and a browser.

▶ No software has to be installed on a device for you to be able to use SAP Fiori. It is a "zero footprint" software.

▶ Personalization is easy: each user's home page can be tailored to complement his daily activities/behavior. This considerably curtails the amount of non-productive navigation that a user would otherwise have to do.

▶ Users can search for apps in a convenient way. A powerful search engine helps in delivering accurate results.

▶ There is a misperception that the launchpad opens up all the data in the connected (back-end) SAP system. Actually, what is visible to a user upon logging into the launchpad is directly controlled by his roles and profiles in the connected system. Therefore, a user only sees what he is authorized for. This has the added advantage of minimizing distractions and "window shopping" for items that incite curiosity only because they are visible.

▶ The SAP Fiori launchpad helps you to navigate intelligently by remembering some important contextual information or navigation states and based on that information, it suggests what could be a next logical step.

▶ Because SAP Fiori apps are device-agnostic, the launchpad adjusts its dimensions to any device that you are using. The launchpad therefore looks the same on a desktop as it does on an iPad. This also ensures that you do not need to worry about what information on the screen may have potentially been cut off. Figure 8.1 shows how a typical SAP Fiori launchpad renders on a desktop/laptop.

Figure 8.1: SAP Fiori launchpad on a desktop

Now let's see how the same launchpad renders on the iPad. This is shown in Figure 8.2.

Figure 8.2: SAP Fiori launchpad on a tablet

As you can see when you compare the same launchpad screen on both a desktop and a tablet, it looks exactly the same on both devices.

8.3   Launching the launchpad

You can start the launchpad by navigating to the URL given to you by your Basis administrator. Once you type this URL into your browser address bar, the launchpad is displayed. Alternatively, if the SAP Fiori launchpad application is on your desktop or in the user menu of your device, you can launch it via the corresponding icon. In each case, a logon screen for validation of your credentials appears, as shown in Figure 8.3.

Regardless of whether you are an end user or administrator, you will need to access SAP Fiori from the launchpad. Once you are in the launchpad, the apps that you have authorization for are displayed (based on roles and profiles assigned to you in the underlying SAP system) in the form of tiles, as shown in Figure 8.4.

Figure 8.3: Launchpad logon screen

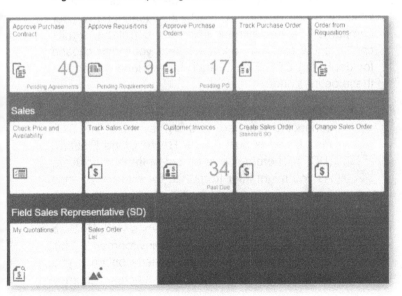

Figure 8.4: Tiled display of apps in the launchpad

You can customize the look and feel of the launchpad. You can create a new group by clicking + next to ADD GROUP (as shown in Figure 8.5) and then giving it an appropriate name.

Figure 8.5: Adding a new group in the launchpad

In this example, I added a new group called **Supervisor**. I can delete it if I want to.

8.4 SAP Fiori launchpad deployment options

At the time of writing this book, there are four ways in which you can deploy the SAP Fiori launchpad in your company. The deployment approach correlates significantly to the technical approach that you have chosen for deploying SAP Fiori overall. Let us look at each of these options briefly:

► Option 1: You can use the SAP Fiori Cloud to connect to your back-end SAP systems. The SAP Fiori Cloud is built on the HANA Cloud Platform (HCP). Therefore, it is an out-of-the-box solution. As you might infer from this, the number of apps it comes pre-packaged with is limited to the most popular business scenarios. The good news is that you can enhance existing apps via SAP Web IDE (integrated development environment). This is a most economical and speedy option if you want to start your SAP Fiori launchpad journey quickly. We will look at SAP Web IDE in more detail in Chapter 10.

▶ Option 2: You can subscribe to the HANA Cloud Portal. It too is powered by HCP. You will understandably ask what the difference is between options 1 and 2. The major difference is that option 2 gives you complete control over your launchpad and SAP Fiori apps because you are essentially creating a new website with SAP Fiori apps that are embedded in the portal.

▶ Option 3: This is the traditional option of deploying SAP Fiori on-premise on a server. Obviously, it works well if your SAP footprint is on-premise. Clearly, this is not a "quick and dirty" option because significant legwork is necessary, including setting up a separate SAP NetWeaver Gateway server for SAP Fiori.

▶ Option 4: The final option that I am proposing here is to embed the launchpad in your Enterprise Portal. However, this option comes with a few restrictions. Firstly, you must have SAP Enterprise Portal running in your business to use this option. Secondly, certain aspects of the Portal may not be interoperable with the launchpad, thereby leading to some unpredictable results.

▶ In this chapter, we looked at the details of interacting with SAP Fiori through the launchpad— the SAP Fiori portal and the single point of entry to the world of SAP Fiori. If you are a business user, you will be spending a lot of time on the launchpad, so hopefully this chapter has provided you with all the information you need for productive interaction with SAP Fiori.

9 SAP Screen Personas

In Chapter 3, we discussed the concept of personalization at length. We also looked at how SAP has realized personalization over the years. I confined my discussion to traditional SAP GUI-based personalization. In this chapter, I present a modern method of personalization in SAP systems—SAP Screen Personas. This method has become quite popular in the last couple of years. Even if this concept is entirely new to you, I'm sure the word "personas" itself is a fair indication of what the purpose might be: yes, personalization! Read on.

9.1 Overview

I talk to a lot of SAP customers regularly and it's clear to me that there is some confusion between SAP Fiori and SAP Screen Personas. This is not entirely surprising. In a lot of areas, SAP provides multiple or at least two options for doing more or less the same thing. One good example of this is financial planning, and even today there are many complementary options that customers can choose from, such as Business Planning and Consolidation (BPC), Business Planning & Simulation (or BPS, part of SAP's Strategic Enterprise Management suite), and Integrated Planning (IP).

Sometimes this multiplicity is accidental, and at other times it is by design. And what might seem like "options" for SAP tend to be viewed as confusing by customers. Therefore, if you compare SAP Fiori and SAP Screen Personas, they have a lot in common but also many differences.

The genesis of SAP Screen Personas was the eternal need of SAP customers for a friendlier and more productive end-user experience. With SAP Screen Personas, as the name might suggest, you can personalize standard SAP GUI screens based on the way you interact with SAP when executing your business processes. Launched commercially at the end of 2012, the whole idea is to make it easy for business users to personalize the screens that they commonly use with relatively minimal code in order to streamline the interaction as follows: by limiting the number of fields to only those where data input is necessary; reducing the amount of repetitive, manual effort by intelligently pre-populating data in previously used fields; and customizing the look and feel to meet the respective user's sense of aesthetics. At the time of writing this book, the latest version of SAP Screen Personas is 3.0. The major difference between this version and the previous one (2.0) is that 3.0 works across all SAP landscapes, while 2.0 only worked for the ECC landscape. At present, SAP Screen Personas allows customization of over 10,000 Web Dynpro screens in ECC. If there is one key thing to note about this tool, it is this: it is all about empowering business users with the means to hide standard SAP fields irrelevant to them.

So from the very start, you can sense the similarities and also possibly some differences. Let's look at them in a more structured way, delving into some of the specific areas of customization, fewer clicks, and a better overall end user experience:

- ▶ Reduction in the number of tabs on an SAP transaction screen that you have to click your way through
- ▶ Minimization of hierarchies and the attendant expanding of nodes to find the function or option you are looking for

▶ Minimization and potential elimination of redundant pushbuttons that are of no relevance to you

▶ Better usage of available screen "real estate"; unnecessary white space can be purged; adequate space can be provided for "memo" type fields

9.2 Similarities and differences between SAP Fiori and SAP Screen Personas

Let us now look at the similarities and differences between these two technologies.

The similarities are:

▶ The key driver for both technologies is a better end user experience

▶ Both technologies are role-based/profile-based, that is, screens can be adapted to the role/profile a user has in an SAP system

▶ Both technologies are intrinsically "free", meaning that both are bundled into your standard SAP license set and are not treated as add-on packages with additional license fees

The differences are:

▶ Every GUI-based SAP transaction can be converted into a screen persona; not every SAP transaction can be converted into an SAP Fiori app

▶ SAP Fiori works on mobile devices; SAP Screen Personas is desktop-based

Development and enhancement in SAP Fiori is typically done by developers, whereas customization of SAP Screen Personas is typically done by business users. Now that you have seen the similarities and differences between the two applications, you must be wondering whether there are any rules of thumb on how to decide which application to choose. The answer is yes! SAP provides you with basic decision criteria to help you make this decision. Figure 9.1 shows a simple decision tree for determining when it makes sense to choose SAP Fiori and when to choose SAP Screen Personas.

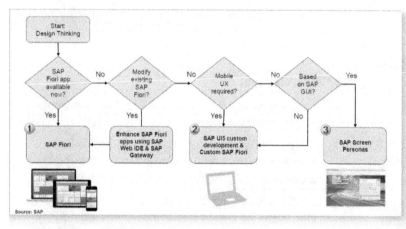

Figure 9.1: Decision tree for choosing between SAP Fiori and SAP Screen Personas (source: SAP)

More information on SAP Screen Personas

SAP provides a rapid-deployment solution for SAP Screen Personas 3.0. Two of the most popular websites on SAP Screen Personas are: *https://rapid.sap. com/bp/#/RDS_PERSO* and *https://wiki. scn.sap.com/wiki/display/Img/SAPScreenPersonas*.

10 Custom SAP Fiori development and enhancements

After taking a slight detour with SAP Screen Personas, we are ready to get back on the SAP Fiori highway. In this chapter, I present how to build custom SAP Fiori apps and extend existing SAP Fiori apps. Although SAP now provides over 500 SAP Fiori apps, you can either extend these apps or create new apps using a (relatively) new SAP development platform called SAP Web Integrated Development Environment (SAP Web IDE). A lot of customers that have implemented SAP Fiori are starting to extend standard SAP Fiori apps. Building a brand new app using SAP Fiori is more difficult than extending an existing one. Thankfully, SAP makes the task of extending an existing app less painful by providing all the necessary templates. It also provides the right kind of accelerators, such as good documentation, code snippets, videos, etc.

However, before we jump into SAP Web IDE, let's look at why we would need to extend an SAP Fiori app.

10.1 Why do you need to extend SAP Fiori apps?

What are the business drivers for extending an SAP Fiori app? Here are some of the most common ones:

▶ Your user community has been using the standard SAP Fiori app for a while and is now asking for additional features—this situation is analogous to any software application: once users are comfortable with it, they ask for more.

▶ You want to further enhance the end user experience. Your users probably need more "bells and whistles" on the user interface—things like a list of items here and a logo there. If you handle this smartly, this can become your company-branded interface.

▶ Your organization (which has already been using SAP and SAP Fiori for a while) has recently had an influx of new users and these users have never worked with SAP software before. This is actually a fairly common scenario in the world of mergers and acquisitions. Company A (an SAP customer) acquires Company B (not an SAP customer). It is natural to expect Company B personnel to be hesitant about using SAP. The situation could get worse if Company B does not find the SAP user experience as engaging as their past experiences with other applications. Rolling out and extending SAP Fiori apps will most likely increase user adoption as these new users perceive these apps to be less intertwined with SAP.

10.2 Skill sets needed for SAP Web IDE development

Web IDE development skillsets

 Building new SAP Fiori apps or extending existing apps requires skill sets that are quite different to traditional SAP skills. Many companies (mistakenly) feel that existing traditional SAP ABAP-centric skillsets are sufficient for development in Web IDE. There are many more skillsets that will be needed to leverage the considerable potential of Web IDE.

Developing SAP Fiori apps and/or customizing them requires the following skill-sets as a minimum: Java development

- ▶ HTML5 development
- ▶ CSS3 development
- ▶ User interface (UI) design
- ▶ ABAP development skills

The first three (technical) skill sets are necessary for the coding work that has to be done. The work that these developers will do can be viewed as front-end development activities. For the developers to be successful in not only meeting the user requirements but also delivering a superior user experience, in a way that ensures that users want to keep coming back, it is recommended that you have at least one user interface design specialist on your SAP Fiori team.

10.3 SAP Web IDE: Introduction

Formerly known as HANA River, *SAP Web IDE* is a development environment that runs on SAP HANA and allows you to build applications using SAP's UI5 (or HTML 5) technology. It is part of the umbrella known as the HANA Cloud Platform. SAP Web IDE is a web-based comprehensive development environment in that you can not only design but also develop, test, and deploy these applications on various devices including mobile devices. In other words, you can build an application that will render the same way regardless of the presentation medium. SAP Web IDE empowers users to build and customize SAP Fiori applications with minimal effort using templates, wizards, and extensive drag-and-drop features.

Note that SAP provides users of this environment with some basic "accelerators" to get them started. Those of you who are familiar with or have used SAP Business Warehouse (BW) will be familiar with *standard business content*—which is SAP terminology for pre-packaged BW content for technical personnel to use as a reference or building block. In the case of SAP Fiori, SAP provides the following reference apps as part of the SAP Web IDE environment:

▶ Approve purchase orders
▶ Manage products
▶ Shop

10.4 Accessing the SAP HANA Cloud Platform

To access SAP Web IDE, you need an account in the SAP HANA Cloud Platform. No sweat! These days, SAP allows free subscription to a lot of their new products. To access SAP Web IDE, navigate to SAP's cloud subscription website at *https://account.hanatrial.ondemand.com*. The screen shown in Figure 10.1 appears.

Figure 10.1: SAP HANA Cloud Platform

This platform is a multi-purpose development platform and you can build and deploy any conceivable application that you can think of on HANA (in the cloud). SAP Fiori is one of the types of applications that you can develop.

If you do not already have an account you will need to register. Once you register, you will receive an online notification.

Click CONTINUE to create your developer account. Once your developer account has been created (a matter of a few seconds), the *SAP HANA Cloud Platform Cockpit* appears. Initially, it will seem a little overwhelming, especially for those of you who are used to the conventional SAP ABAP-based development media. Be forewarned, SAP Web IDE looks nothing like the ABAP development workbench nor is it meant to.

In the SAP HANA Cloud Platform Cockpit, all the functions that are available to you are contained in the navigation menu on the left-hand side. Figure 10.2 shows what you could expect to see.

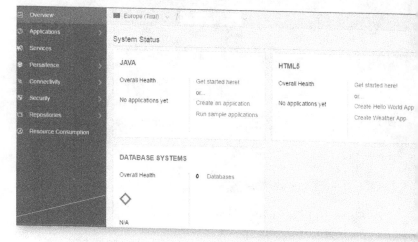

Figure 10.2: SAP HANA Cloud Platform Cockpit

The OVERVIEW screen includes a dashboard containing information about the overall health of the system. If you are just starting your SAP Web IDE journey, I strongly recommend that you click the GET STARTED HERE! link or the links below this in the JAVA or the HTML5 panels. Within this chapter we are interested in extending an SAP Fiori app and therefore you might want to start with HTML5.

Click APPLICATIONS in the navigation menu to expand the node. You can drill down into the four sub-items as shown in Figure 10.3.

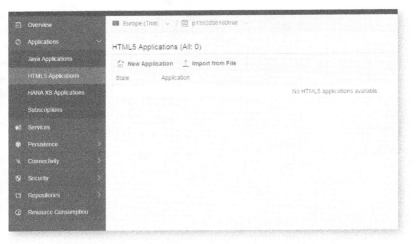

Figure 10.3: Applications in SAP Web IDE

Now let's look at the SERVICES item in the navigation menu because this is where you will be able to subscribe to any service that you need to use for building or expanding applications. For those of you interested in the technical aspects, it is useful to know that SAP Web IDE works on the concept of services. As a designer/developer, you will need to subscribe to a particular service.

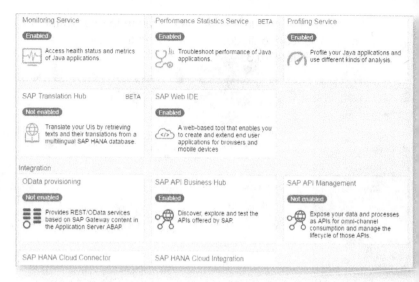

Figure 10.4: Extract of services

Figure 10.4 shows some of the services that are available for subscription. Those services that you have enabled will show up as ENABLED.

Now let's look at the PERSISTENCE item in the navigation menu. What is the importance of persistence? If you want your application and data to be stored on a particular database or become part of a service request, this is where you will start. Figure 10.5 shows the PERSISTENCE function with the DATABASE SYSTEMS option selected.

Because no database systems have been set up yet, nothing is listed. Click DATABASES & SCHEMAS and then the NEW button. You can now create a new schema, assigning it a name and a database.

Figure 10.5: Snapshot of persistence

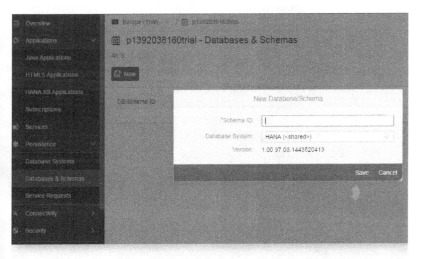

Figure 10.6: Creating a new database/schema

Figure 10.6 shows how to create a new database/ schema. For now, click CANCEL and then SERVICE RE-QUESTS in the navigation menuu on the left and then the NEW REQUEST button. The dialog box shown in Figure 10.7 appears.

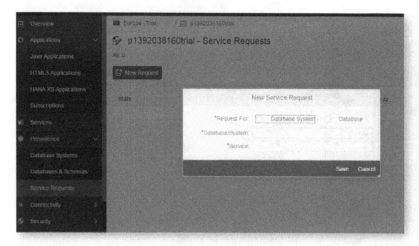

Figure 10.7: Creating a new service request

On this screen you have to provide all the mandatory information in order to create a valid service request. For now, we will click CANCEL and continue with our basic navigation in the SAP Web IDE environment.

Now let's click on the next item in the navigation menu, CONNECTIVITY, to expand the node. By clicking the sub-item DESTINATIONS, you can display a list of destinations that your account is currently configured for.

Figure 10.8: Maintaining destinations for your account

You can create a new destination by clicking NEW DESTI-
NATION or alternatively, import an existing destination by
clicking IMPORT DESTINATION (see Figure 10.8). At this
point in time, you can ignore the CLOUD CONNECTORS
menu item because it is of limited importance to you.

We will now shift our attention to an important function in
the SAP Web IDE environment: security. This area is
particularly important if you work in the area of security
or auditing. Click SECURITY to expand the node and show
the three sub-items in the menu. Figure 10.9 shows a
screenshot with the TRUST sub-item selected.

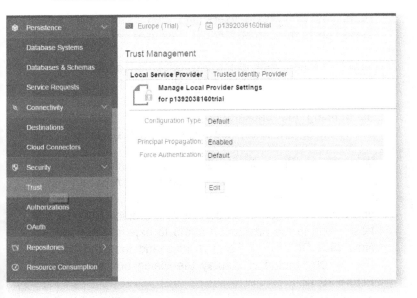

Figure 10.9: Security configuration in SAP Web IDE

On this screen, you can change key parameters. Clicking AUTHORIZATIONS in the navigation menu displays the
screen shown in Figure 10.10.

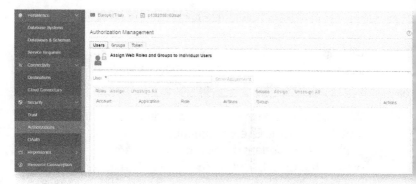

Figure 10.10: Authorizations management in SAP Web IDE

Here, you can create users and then assign roles to these users. You can also create new user groups.

Now let's take a look at the final option under SECURITY, OAUTH. Here, you perform cosmetic tasks that are connected to the branding of your SAP Fiori screens, such as defining the background, logo, etc. Figure 10.11 shows the area where you would perform this activity.

We will now turn our attention to documentation. SAP Web IDE allows you to create document repositiories where you can create and store all the documents that you have put together as part of your project. Click RE- POSITORIES in the navigation menu to expand the node. Now click DOCUMENT REPOSITORIES and then the NEW REPOSITORY button to display the dialog box shown in Figure 10.12.

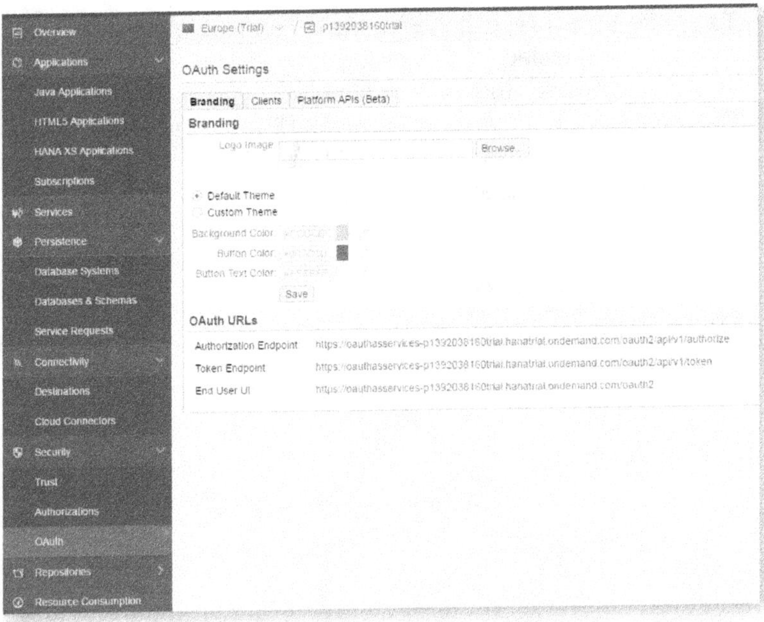

Figure 10.11: Branding activities in SAP Web IDE

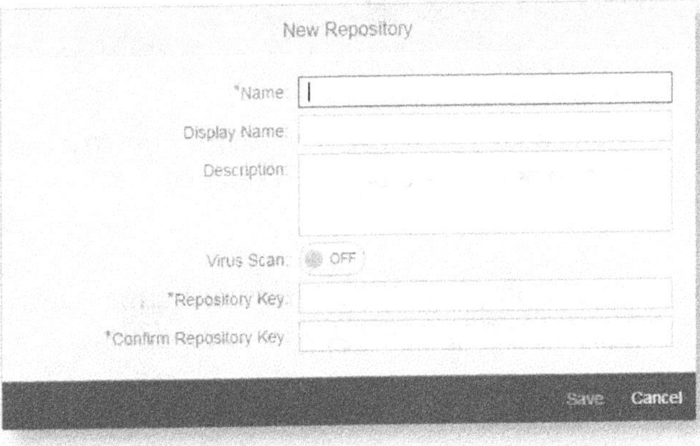

Figure 10.12: Creating a new document repository

To create a new repository, you have to provide the information requested in the dialog box. If you want to create a Git repository, you can do so by clicking GIT REPOSITORIES in the navigation menu. For those of you who are not familiar with Git and GitHub, this is a version management application that helps you manage all artifacts for a project. When you click GIT REPOSITORIES, a dialog box appears where you have to enter the name of the repository as the starting point. This is shown in Figure 10.13.

Figure 10.13: Creating a new Git repository

We are now ready to use SAP Web IDE to create a new SAP Fiori app or modify a pre-delivered app.

10.5 Leveraging SAP Web IDE to enhance a pre-delivered SAP Fiori app

Let us return to the SERVICES item in the menu. Click this item to expand the node and then scroll down until you find the SAP WEB IDE service. This is shown in Figure 10.14.

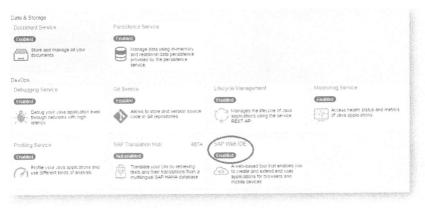

Figure 10.14: SAP Web IDE service in the SAP HANA Cloud Platform Cockpit

Because we had already enabled the SAP Web IDE service, you can now click on the SAP WEB IDE hyperlink. It will take you to the web page shown in Figure 10.15.

Figure 10.15: Important SAP Web IDE links

Now click the OPEN SAP WEB IDE hyperlink and once SAP Web IDE has loaded, the next screen appears.This screen is shown in Figure 10.16.

Figure 10.16: SAP Web IDE landing page

As you can see, there are four options that you can choose from to create a project:

1. Quick Start with Layout Editor

2. New Project from Template

3. New Project from Sample Application

4. New Extension Project

As someone new to this environment, the pragmatic approach for you will be to select option (3). Selecting this option takes you to the screen shown in Figure 10.17.

This book is not meant to be a technical "how to" manual, so I will just walk you through the templates that you will encounter during the process of creating or modifying your app.

Figure 10.17: Creating or modifying an app in SAP Web IDE

SAP Web IDE & the Model View Controller paradigm

 For those of you with a technical mindset, SAP Web IDE development follows the *Model View Controller (MVC)* approach. The guiding principle of this modular approach is that the business logic is separated from the user interface and both of these are separate from the implementation of the business logic.

The purchase order (PO) approval project contains multiple template files that will help you to extend this application. Let's start with the CSS template shown in Figure 10.18. For this application, this file is called **approve POStyle.css**. You can make any changes you want and then save them.

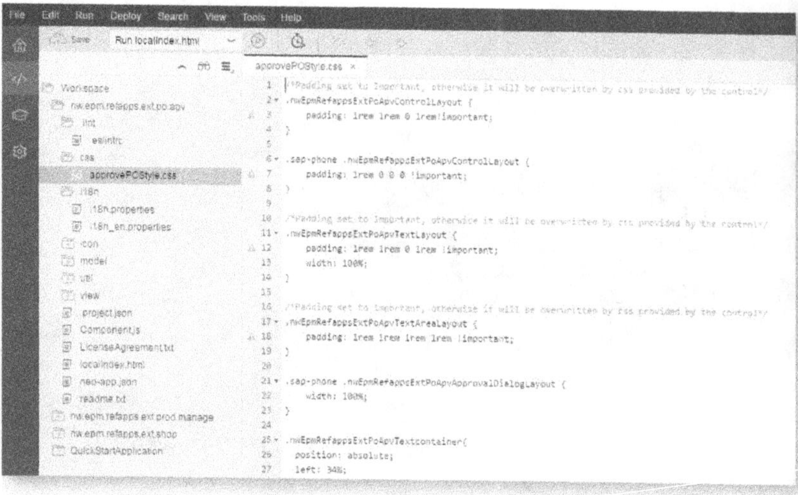

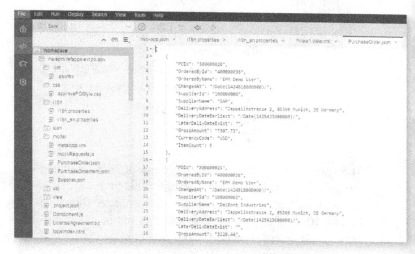

Figure 10.18: CSS template for PO approval

Figure 10.19 shows the **i18** file. You can make whatever changes you want to your text.

Figure 10.19: Standard i18 file for the PO approval app

The **icon** folder is generated by default and contains files that control the rendering of your app on the various media. Figure 10.20 shows the contents of this folder.

Figure 10.20: Contents of the icon folder for the PO approval app

The **model** folder contains files that allow you to modify the purchase order approval model. It corresponds to the *model* component of the MVC concept. This component has the relevant files that determine what the purchase order approval model will look like. You can make changes or add additional POs with their relevant details in one or more of these files. Figure 10.21 shows the corresponding **json** file for the header.

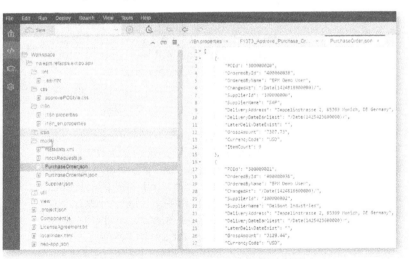

Figure 10.21: The standard PO approval json model

Figure 10.22 shows a partial screenshot of the *PO approval json model* for the PO items.

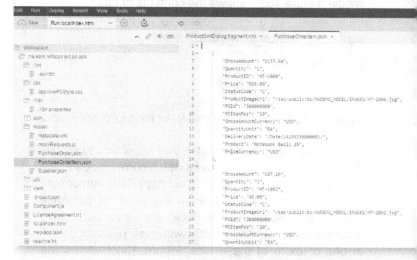

Figure 10.22: The standard PO approval json template for line items

The next folder we are going to take a look at is the **util** folder. This folder consists of files that help you enhance ancillary functionality in this PO approval app. Figure 10.23 shows the pre-delivered contents of the **approver.js** file.

The contents in the next folder (**view**) directly correspond to the view component in the MVC model. A PO has a summarized and a detailed view. SAP provides standard templates for both views in both .xml and JavaScript notations. If you want to modify the standard view of this app, you will need to modify one or more of these files. Figure 10.24 shows the .xml file for the PO view.

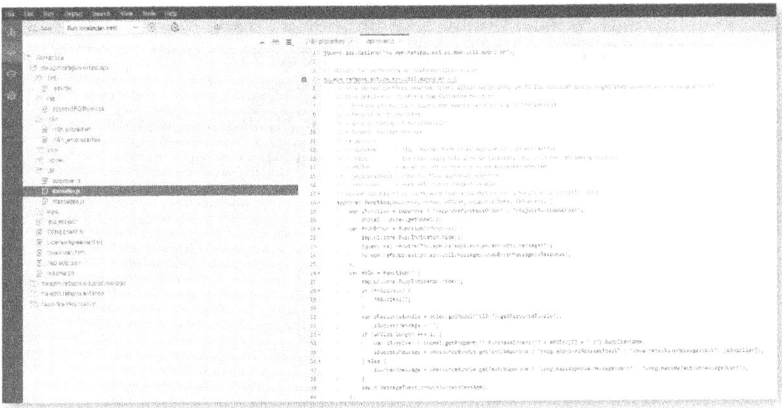

Figure 10.23: Standard approver.js file for the PO approval app

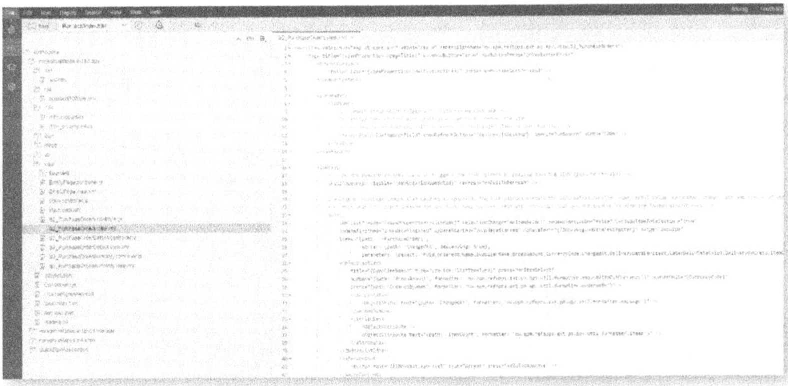

Figure 10.24: Standard xml template for the PO approval view

The standard template for each app contains many other folders and files but I will not address each of these in detail. As explained earlier, they are of interest only if you (as a developer) are planning on modifying an existing app or creating a new one. A detailed treatment of this topic would fill an entire book and is not in scope for this publication.

We have now completed our technical deep dive into SAP Fiori and are ready to take a business-centric and requirements-centric approach to SAP Fiori. We will do this in Chapter 11 and put together a business case for introducing SAP Fiori in your organization.

11 Putting together an SAP Fiori business case for your organization

You are now hopefully familiar with the technical aspects of SAP Fiori. It is therefore time to switch gears from theory to practice and bring together everything you have learned in the past ten chapters to transform this acquired knowledge into one or more tangible outcomes. In other words, you are now ready to introduce SAP Fiori into your organization and take the first steps towards doing so. So what are the things that are important to key decision-makers and stakeholders in a way that would make them want to invest in this new technology? In this chapter, I familiarize you with the points you should consider when putting together an SAP Fiori business case.

11.1 What gaps can SAP Fiori potentially fill?

Table 11.1 lists complaints commonly heard about standard SAP screens (generally, SAP GUI) and details how SAP Fiori seeks to address each of these complaints. You can use this information as a basic guide for building a business case for SAP Fiori.

Challenge/complaint	SAP Fiori response/solution
Dissatisfaction with current SAP user interface	SAP Fiori was introduced to provide users with a superior user experience
Navigation on current SAP screens is difficult	SAP Fiori provides easy and intuitive navigation
Customization and enhancement of standard SAP screens is difficult	With SAP Web IDE, SAP Fiori allows you to customize, personalize, and extend standard SAP screens to meet any user's specific needs
The same SAP screen renders differently on different devices, making for an inconsistent user experience	SAP Fiori apps are device-agnostic; because they are built using HTML5 technologies, there is a standard, consistent user experience regardless of the device
Starting an SAP transaction with a transaction code or clicking through menus is not optimal	SAP Fiori organizes your menu in the form of Windows tiles; there is no need to enter a transaction code or click through menus
Customization of standard SAP screens typically involves using a third party product which means additional license & consulting costs	SAP does not charge an extra fee for SAP Fiori
Standard SAP screens need a fair amount of "change management", especially for users who are new to the SAP standard interface	SAP Fiori does not require any training: the apps are user-friendly enough to be self-explanatory

Table 11.1: How SAP Fiori addresses some complaints commonly heard about traditional SAP user interfaces

11.2 Customer (ABC) background

In this section, I will introduce you to the considerations and work that went into creating a business case for SAP Fiori for a Fortune 500 customer. The objective of this section is to help you formulate similar business cases in your respective organizations using my experiences and lessons learned as a useful basis.

Customer ABC

 Customer ABC is a Fortune 500 manufacturing company with over $10 billion in annual revenues, has operations in over 30 countries, and has 20,000 employees worldwide. SAP is the system of record for all supply chain transaction data. (Note that ABC is a fictitious name I will use through the rest of the book but everything else about this case study is real, including the company). However, SAP is by no means the only enterprise application running in the supply chain space. The company uses many legacy systems which feed data to SAP and in some cases, these legacy systems receive information from SAP. To make things a little more complicated, ABC has an insatiable appetite for acquisitions and each time there is an acquisition, new systems are added to the landscape.

ABC is one of the thousands of SAP customers that have often been upset, frustrated, but mostly disappointed that they have had to conduct their daily business over many years via "those gray screens" with literally hundreds of fields that they have had to navigate through for very little reason. Because this company has a plethora of non-SAP applications, it has been exposed to a whole gamut of user-friendly applications over many years. They have therefore found it hard to accept that there is not a more pleasant way of interacting with their SAP environment. Quite a few SAP workarounds have been tried out to provide a more streamlined and pleasant user experience and some at considerable cost, but so far, these workarounds have had transient impacts at the most. My personal experience of having worked on these third party SAP GUI simplification tools is that they do not represent a new user interface and are built on the standard SAP GUI, so the overall experience is not much different.

Enter SAP Fiori: like a lot of customers and clients I have worked with, ABC first came across SAP Fiori at an SAP conference. They were very impressed but since it was 2013, they—like a lot of other customers I know of—were told that they would have to pay for SAP Fiori licenses. Because ABC had many other priorities, they decided not to go through the entire exercise of business case justification. They also felt that even if they had the time to create the business case, they would not have done so on principle because they had expected—like a lot of customers I know—that something like SAP Fiori would be available to download free of charge from the SAP Service Marketplace, just like a new version of SAP GUI.

11.3 Selecting an SAP Fiori use case

Once ABC was introduced to SAP Fiori, there was obviously a lot of excitement. However, as with any new software, the initial buzz can be quickly followed by disappointment if expectations are not met meaningfully at the very outset. Therefore, it is important to consider some key criteria before determining whether your organization is ready for SAP Fiori. Let's look at the important issues:

▶ Has your organization been running SAP for a considerable period of time? By "considerable", I mean at least five years or more. If it has, you have probably been using the standard SAP user conduits such as SAP GUI, Web GUI, and NetWeaver Business Client. This means that introducing SAP Fiori would potentially entail managing change because SAP Fiori represents a very different way of interacting with SAP. If your organization is relatively new to SAP or considering implementing it for the first time, you will be able to establish SAP Fiori in your organization a lot more smoothly because there is very little to compare with. It is natural that the longer you are used to doing things a certain way, the harder it is to embrace something new. It is therefore not uncommon to see mature SAP enterprises finding it harder to introduce SAP Fiori in their organizations.

▶ Is your workforce fairly mobile? SAP Fiori is an appropriate choice for organizations with personnel that needs to conduct business via multiple devices, including mobile ones. SAP Fiori has the most impact and effect on mobile devices. For those workers that are fairly static, SAP Fiori would at best be treated as an attractive alternative to the conventional software.

▶ What is the overall satisfaction level with the conventional modes of user interaction with SAP in your organization? If it is low to medium, then this could be a key driver to introducing SAP Fiori. If users are generally satisfied, then you would need to build a more compelling case for SAP Fiori.

▶ Does your organization have the technical skill sets that are required for SAP Fiori? In Chapter 10 I covered the key skill sets necessary. Development in SAP Fiori is quite different to the traditional ABAP-based SAP development approach. If you do not have the kinds of skill sets needed for SAP Fiori, your organization will have a hard time maintaining and enhancing it. However, this should not be a major showstopper—you can fill this knowledge gap by hiring or contracting.

11.4 Searching for the relevant app

Now that SAP has a very large collection of SAP Fiori apps that is likely to get even larger, it also provides you with a convenient way to search for an app. You can access the SAP Fiori apps reference library home page at *https://fioriappslibrary.hana.ondemand.com/sap/fix/externalViewer/#/home* (see Figure 11.1).

As you may surmise from Figure 11.1, you can search for apps in a variety of ways. SAP makes the search easy by providing various filters. For example, if you know the industry sector to which the app you are searching for belongs, simply click By Industry to display a list of industries, some of which are shown on the left-hand side in Figure 11.2.

Figure 11.1: Searching for an app in the SAP Fiori apps reference library

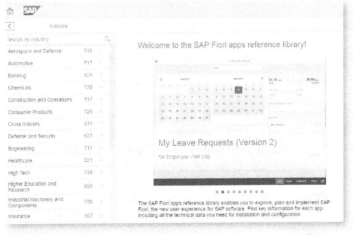

Figure 11.2: List of SAP Fiori apps by industry

127

Looking at the number of apps per industry gives you an idea of how many business processes SAP has enabled for SAP Fiori.

My favorite way to search for SAP Fiori apps is by using the BY BACK-END PRODUCT filter. I like it because I usually know the application component or module the app belongs to. Figure 11.3 shows a partial screenshot of a search filtered by back-end product.

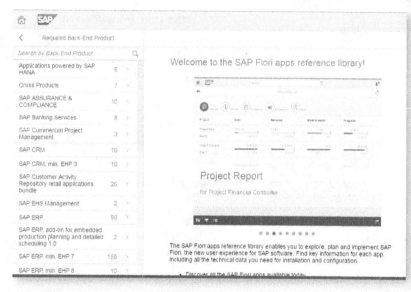

Figure 11.3: SAP Fiori apps by back-end product

Note that your screen may not look exactly like the one shown here. This is because SAP updates the content frequently, meaning that new apps are added with each release/wave. However, you should see the categories on the left-hand side of the screen. You can browse through the apps by expanding each node. This gives you a rather comprehensive view of the apps at your disposal.

Let us assume you want to look for the purchase order approval app. In the search field, enter **purchase orders** to run a rather generic search. Figure 11.4 shows the few hits returned by this search.

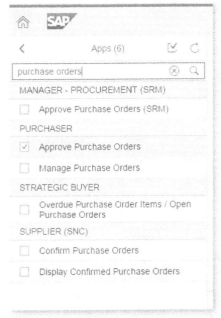

Figure 11.4: Hit list of purchase order SAP Fiori apps

Click the magnifying glass icon in Figure 11.4 to display the list of purchase order apps. The **Approve Purchase Orders** app is listed. Select the app to display relevant information in the right-hand panel as shown in Figure 11.5.

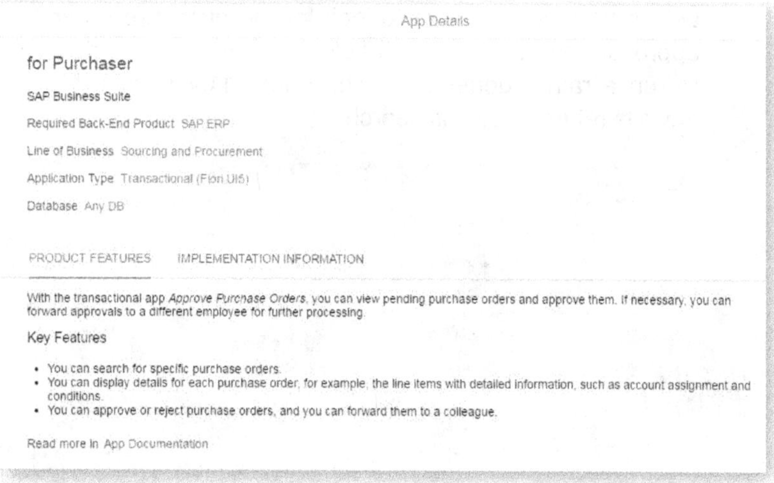

App Details

for Purchaser

SAP Business Suite

Required Back-End Product SAP ERP

Line of Business Sourcing and Procurement

Application Type Transactional (Fiori UI5)

Database Any DB

PRODUCT FEATURES   IMPLEMENTATION INFORMATION

With the transactional app *Approve Purchase Orders*, you can view pending purchase orders and approve them. If necessary, you can forward approvals to a different employee for further processing.

Key Features

- You can search for specific purchase orders.
- You can display details for each purchase order, for example, the line items with detailed information, such as account assignment and conditions.
- You can approve or reject purchase orders, and you can forward them to a colleague.

Read more in App Documentation

Figure 11.5: Basic information about the purchase order approval app

All the information relevant to the APPROVE PURCHASE ORDER app is available here. The PRODUCT FEATURES tab contains basic information about this app, including its main features. The IMPLEMENTATION INFORMATION tab contains the technical details, including installation, configuration, extensibility, and support information.

11.5 Implementing the SAP Fiori business case

Once the decision had been taken to implement APPROVE PURCHASE ORDERS for ABC, we checked the prerequisites for the app on the SAP Help Portal. It is important to note that at the time of writing this book, SAP Fiori apps can be run in one of two ways: either on any database (but not including SAP HANA) or on SAP HANA. This demo will be for the latter option because the SAP transaction system is SAP Business Suite on SAP HANA. This app was delivered by SAP in Q3 2015.

The technical prerequisites are as follows:

Back-end

You must be on one of the following ERP Enhancement Packages and/or Support Package Stacks on your back-end to be able to implement this app:

▶ EHP2 FOR SAP ERP 6.0 – SPS 05

▶ EHP3 FOR SAP ERP 6.0 – SPS 05

▶ EHP4 FOR SAP ERP 6.0 – SPS 05

▶ EHP4 FOR SAP ERP 6.0 / NW7.01 – SPS 05

▶ EHP5 FOR SAP ERP 6.0 – SPS 03

▶ EHP6 FOR SAP ERP 6.0 – SPS 01

▶ EHP7 FOR SAP ERP 6.0 – SPS 01

▶ SAP ERP 6.0 – SPS 15 (02/2009)

Front-end

You must be on at least SAP Fiori version 1.0 for SAP ERP.

11.6 SAP Fiori deployment options

You essentially have two options for deploying your SAP Fiori app: *buy* versus *build*. In understanding each of these options, it is important to realize that with the **buy** option, you are not buying any new software. The decision really hinges on the expertise available—that is, whether you want to deploy your first SAP Fiori app in-house or you want to engage external services/consulting to do this for you. Similarly, when I say

build, you may not actually be building a new app but rather performing all activities that would enable your business to utilize your first SAP Fiori app. From that perspective, this option could be called **self-deploy**. It would be a real "build" if you were designing and developing an SAP Fiori app from scratch. Let's look at each of these options in more detail.

Buy

The smartest way to buy is to utilize the rapid-deployment solutions (RDS) that SAP and its partners offer. Some consulting companies may not call this service a rapid-deployment solution but the goal is to provide your organization with a head start on your SAP Fiori initiatives. In particular, the SAP rapid-deployment solutions deliver the following:

▶ Dissemination of best practices for SAP Fiori Design, SAP UI5, evaluation of client architecture readiness for SAP Fiori and any installations necessary, reference architecture, etc.

▶ A "Design Thinking Workshop" which includes (but is not limited to) identifying use cases for SAP Fiori, discovery sessions, storyboarding, scope evaluation for the proof of concept, and finalization, etc.

▶ Realization of use case(s): this service focuses on realizing the use case(s) that you have finalized with SAP or its partner during this rapid-deployment solution engagement. This is your proof of concept. SAP will follow its set of templates and methodology to ensure that you the customer are able to leverage SAP's standard approach.

Planning for an SAP Fiori rapid-deployment solution engagement

 A standard SAP Fiori rapid-deployment solution engagement runs for approximately 18–20 days. The engagement is split into different phases. A question that is often asked by organizations that are contemplating engaging such a service is "what kind of time commitment do I need and who should be involved?"

To answer this question, it is important to understand that an SAP Fiori rapid-deployment solution implementation is not a turnkey effort. Neither is it merely a set of technical activities. For your SAP Fiori rapid-deployment solution effort to succeed, you will need to treat it as a joint effort between SAP (or the partner) and you (the customer). Customer participation will be most necessary during workshops and testing. The resources required for these workshops are primarily selected power users (from business) and relevant technology resources. Some level of technical support (primarily during the initial technical evaluation and installation period) and later on during development is recommended.

Build/self-deploy

Should you decide to go with the build option, you have the freedom to set your own scope and to experiment. However, unless you have some in-house expertise with SAP Fiori, you might be flying blind. Although a lot of organizations are "building" their SAP Fiori footprint by means of self-learning, research, and training, I am increasingly observing that they are also engaging some level of external expertise to accelerate things. With this option, you can take any number of days based on what works best for you. The first time you employ the build option it will probably take you longer than a packaged rapid-deployment solution approach would because there is a strong likelihood of trial and error. The flip side is that you will probably learn a lot more than you would with a turnkey approach. The lessons you learn and the insights you glean from your in-house efforts could position you well for your future rollouts.

In this chapter, we looked at the activities involved in conceiving and crystallizing an SAP Fiori business case. You are now ready to move to the next phase in this journey, implementing your selected business case. We will cover this in detail in Chapter 12.

12 Implementing SAP Fiori in your business

In Chapter 11, we looked at how to establish a business case for SAP Fiori. We then looked at the strategic options available for choosing how to potentially proceed. In this chapter, I present an implementation template and the specific activities involved in rolling out the purchase order approval app using the self-deployment method.

12.1 Self-deployment of your SAP Fiori business case

Here, I am recommending the build or self-deploy approach to implement your first SAP Fiori app. The approach is based on a generic view of the activities and effort needed to establish an initial SAP Fiori footprint in any business. However, this should not be considered a "one size fits all" approach. Each organization will have its own set of realities and constraints, meaning that the activities and the duration of these activities will have to be fine-tuned.

After analyzing the business case for ABC (the example used in the previous chapter), together with my team I created a high-level project plan containing the high-level activities, durations, and resources. A summary of this plan is shown in Table 12.1. The figures shown in the "Effort" column are my recommendations allowing for the learning curve.

Phase	Summary	Effort	Resources
Discovery	Evaluation & assessment of SAP landscape for SAP Fiori-readiness. Identification of use cases for SAP Fiori & selection of one use case for the proof of concept	6 days (max.)	▸ A Basis/NetWeaver administrator ▸ Business stakeholders, including power users/subject matter experts from client departments ▸ One or two end users
Design, installation, & configuration	Installation of all the prerequisites (notes, SPs), SAP Fiori installations, configuration activities, etc.	6 days	▸ A Basis/NetWeaver administrator ▸ An SAP security administrator ▸ 1-2 SAP configuration specialists representing the business case/process that has been selected for the implementation ▸ An SAP Web IDE development specialist (optional)
Final preparation & deployment	Testing, data validation, documentation, etc.	3 days	▸ 1–2 power users for testing ▸ A few end users of the app for data validation ▸ An SAP NetWeaver/Basis administrator for support

Table 12.1: Summary of activities for deploying your initial SAP Fiori footprint

We will now take a look at each of the phases and the specific activities involved.

Phase 1: Discovery

In this phase, an infrastructure readiness assessment is conducted. During this assessment, the following activities are performed:

- ▶ Assessment of the SAP landscape and comparison with the requirements for SAP Fiori
- ▶ Documentation of the gaps and creation of a plan for closing the gaps (including applying SAP Notes etc.)
- ▶ Determination of the ECC system that will serve as the source (i.e., development vs. sandbox vs. production)
- ▶ Assessment of options for SAP NetWeaver Gateway installation (i.e., embedded versus hub)
- ▶ SAP Fiori overview workshop
- ▶ Requirements workshop to identify potential use cases for SAP Fiori proof of concept
- ▶ Finalization of (one) use case for realization in the proof of concept
- ▶ Analysis of any configuration activities needed in the back-end SAP system
- ▶ Finalization of audience/user group and specific users for proof of concept

Phase 2: Design, installation, and configuration

This is a phase consisting of primarily technical activities. These include:

- ▶ Installing/configuring SAP NetWeaver Gateway
- ▶ Implementing any SAP Notes that are a prerequisite for SAP Fiori

▶ Configuring the relevant ECC components: typically, these are related to the configuration activities you may need to perform for the use case you have selected for implementing your SAP Fiori app

▶ Ensuring that the relevant data is available in your ECC system for implementing your selected SAP Fiori app (i.e., to realize your use case); if the necessary data is not available, ensure that data is loaded

▶ Setting up the necessary roles and authorizations for SAP Fiori testers and users

▶ Documentation of all the technical steps involved in the installation as well as solution design

Phase 3: Final preparation and deployment

This is the final phase and it is similar to *go live*. The activities involved include:

▶ User acceptance testing of proof of concept by predetermined group of users

▶ Basic data validation: the recommended approach is to run the transaction that the SAP Fiori app represents in your ECC system and then run it using the SAP Fiori interface side-by-side and compare the results

▶ Deployment of the app for the target audience: this is the go live for this proof of concept

▶ Post-go live support for:
  – Any bug fixes and minor modifications
  – User training
  – Documentation of lessons learned and best practices

12.2 Configuring the PO approval app

There are a few configuration steps that have to be performed before you can use the app. A user of this app (i.e., someone who will be approving POs) will not need to perform these configuration steps; they are the reponsibility of the NetWeaver administrator. I describe the steps here for the benefit of technical readers.

Step 1: Activate the gateway service for the app in the (source) SAP NetWeaver system

Run transaction SICF to activate the gateway service. Multiple services will need to be activated. The initial screen of this transaction is shown in Figure 12.1.

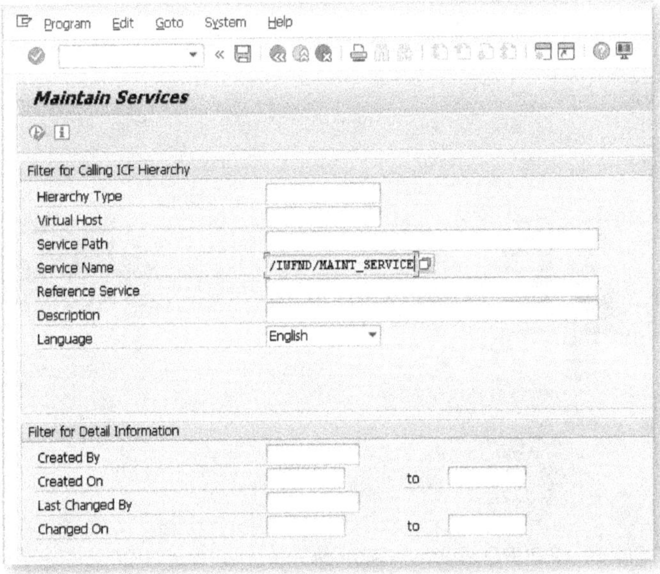

Figure 12.1: Transaction SICF

In the SERVICE NAME field, enter the name of the OData service **/IWFND/MAINT_SERVICE** and then click the EXE-CUTE icon ⊕.

On the SAP NetWeaver Gateway server, you will have to activate the OData (gateway) service. In order to do so, run transaction SICF and then navigate as follows: default_host * SAP • OPU • ODATA • SAP. This will take you to the screen shown in Figure 12.2. In this node, look for the OData service for this particular app. The name is **GBAPP_POAPPROVAL**. Call up the context menu for this entry by clicking the right mouse button. A dialog box appears and if this service is inactive, you can activate it by clicking ACTIVATE SERVICE. Note that if the service is already active, the ACTIVATE SERVICE menu item is disabled so you do not need to do anything.

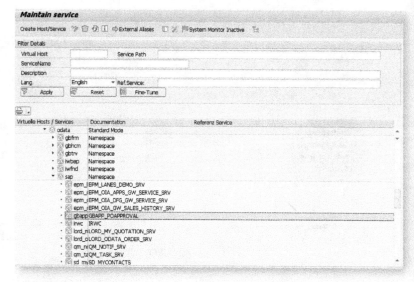

Figure 12.2: PO approval service in transaction SICF

Now double-click the service to go to the maintenance screen for this service. Here, you maintain technical parameters for the service, as shown in Figure 12.3.

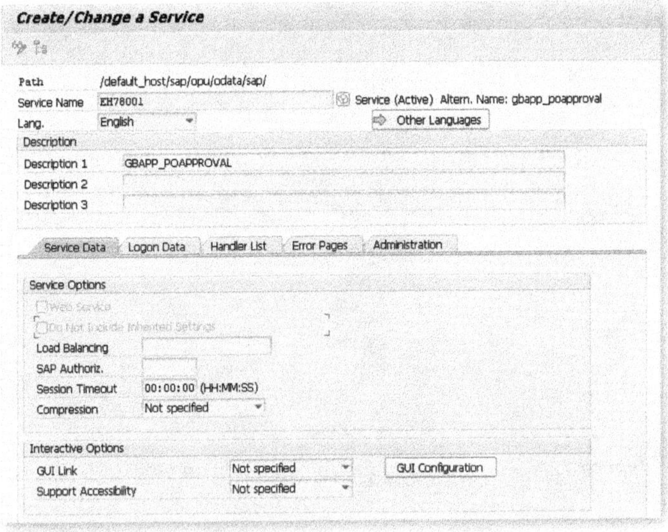

Figure 12.3: Maintaining parameters for the PO approval service

Step 2: Activate the UI5 service in the (source) SAP NetWeaver system

This step is similar to the previous step. The only difference is that this time you activate the UI5 service. In order to do so, in transaction SICF, navigate to SAP • BC • UI5_UI5 • SAP • MM_PO_APV. This is shown in Figure 12.4.

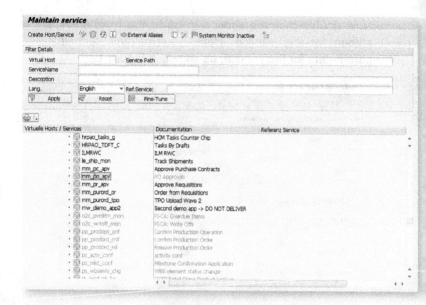

Figure 12.4: Navigating to the relevant UI5 service

With your cursor on the service, click the right mouse button and activate this service by clicking on the first YES button, confirming the activation as shown in Figure 12.5. You will notice a second YES button with a tree icon. If you click this second YES button instead, it will activate not only this service but also all the services underneath it provided they have been maintained. In our case, no sub-services have been maintained for this service, so you can click on either YES button.

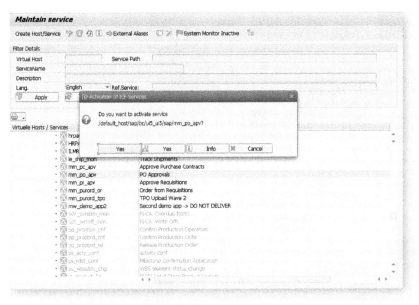

Figure 12.5: Activating the UI5 service

Step 3: Configure user roles for the app in the SAP NetWeaver system

The next step is user role maintenance. This step will be performed by your SAP NetWeaver administrator based on the information you request. However, I will take you through the step here from the perspective of an administrator. In the user maintenance transaction, SU01, enter the relevant user name and then click on the edit icon ✎ as shown in Figure 12.6.

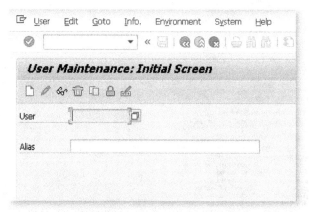

Figure 12.6: User (role) maintenance

The screen shown in Figure 12.7 appears. Any user needing to approve purchase orders using this app must have the following role in their user profile: SAP_MM_PO_APV_APP. On the ROLES tab, enter the role **SAP_MM_PO_APV_APP** and save the information as shown. If this role is already available in this user's user profile you do not need to do anything.

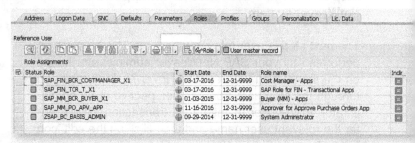

Figure 12.7: Assigning the correct role to the SAP Fiori user

Step 4: Assign the relevant user to the appropriate role for the SAP Fiori launchpad

Each SAP Fiori app has a role associated with it. In order for you (as the user) to successfully communicate with the back-end transaction SAP system through the SAP Fiori user interface, you require the appropriate role in your profile. Please work with your NetWeaver administrator or SAP security specialist to make sure that this role is assigned to you. In the following, I describe the actions required from the perspective of the administrator/security specialist. To assign the role, run the role maintenance transaction PFCG. The initial screen is shown in Figure 12.8.

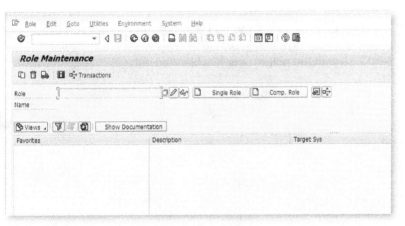

Figure 12.8: Role maintenance in transaction PFCG

In the ROLE field, enter the standard SAP Fiori role as supplied for the purchase order approval app. The technical name for this role is SAP_MM_BCR_Buyer_X1. If you want to browse for this role, click the display icon to go to the role maintenance screen details shown in Figure 12.9 and navigate to the MENU tab to find the role.

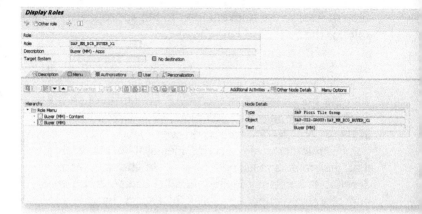

Figure 12.9: Assigning the relevant (buyer) role to an SAP Fiori user (1)

Now go to the USER tab and add the relevant user(s) to the list and save this information. This is shown in Figure 12.10 with the actual user IDs blanked out.

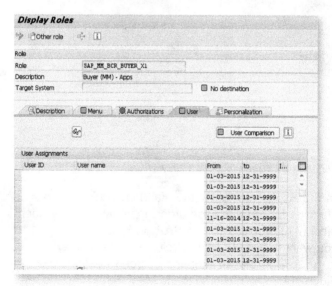

Figure 12.10: Assigning the relevant (buyer) role to an SAP Fiori user (2)

Step 5. Configuration in the ERP system

You will need to perform a few configuration steps in your connected ERP system to make sure that your purchase order approval app works properly. Please note that these customizing steps are only relevant for the PO approval app. In the IMG in your ERP system, navigate to the activity RELEASE PROCEDURE FOR PURCHASE ORDERS via the following path: MATERIALS MANAGEMENT • PURCHASING • PURCHASE ORDER • RELEASE PROCEDURE FOR PURCHASE ORDERS, as shown in Figure 12.11.

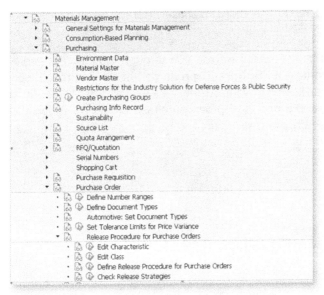

Figure 12.11: App-specific customization in the ERP system

Once the configuration has been completed, you will see the APPROVE PURCHASE ORDERS app as a tile in your SAP Fiori launchpad when you run SAP Fiori, as shown in Figure 12.12.

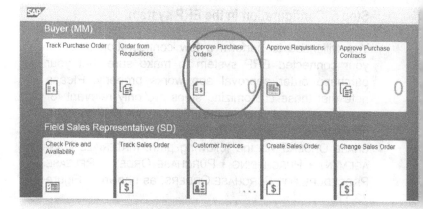

Figure 12.12: Approve Purchase Order app on the SAP Fiori launchpad

In this chapter I walked you through the steps of implementing an SAP Fiori app as part of the first rollout corresponding to your business case. You are now ready to use this app to approve purchase orders for which you have authorization.

13 SAP Fiori implementations— lessons learned

I have been fortunate enough to have implemented SAP Fiori for Fortune 500 organizations. Because my association with SAP Fiori started from the time the product was launched, I have had the privilege of working with a few big customers to guide them through their first ever SAP Fiori implementations. Below is a list of lessons learned and best practices that I hope will help you in your SAP Fiori odyssey. I hope you find them helpful in making your SAP Fiori journey or transition (as the case may be) a smooth one.

▶ Do not approach SAP Fiori as an IT project/initiative. Your chances of success with SAP Fiori will be greatly reduced if you take an IT-centric view. SAP Fiori should be introduced and socialized in every organization as a business-centric initiative. As such, the primary sponsor for SAP Fiori should be one of your business units/departments, preferably Finance. Why Finance? Ultimately, it is the Finance department that holds the purse strings in any organization and to have them fully vested in this initiative will ensure success.

▶ Like every project or initiative, SAP Fiori requires the steadfast support of stakeholders. If there are any naysayers or even fence-sitters, try to identify them at the earliest and make sure you take their concerns into account and convert them into supporters.

▶ A lot of consulting companies tend to do a sub-optimal job of presenting a compelling business case for implementing SAP Fiori. Their proposals often simply echo the marketing hype already produced by SAP. A compelling business case will hone in on the business benefits of SAP Fiori and will minimize the technical jargon.

▶ Set aside a sufficient amount of time for "customer engagement" or socialization of the SAP Fiori paradigm. Unfortunately, there are no short-cuts to this; it will take time and patience. Approaching a client (if you are a consulting company) or one of your departments (if you are an employee and are trying to introduce SAP Fiori into your company) without having adequately socialized the concepts of SAP Fiori will not bode well for success. One of my implementations was a prime example of this situation. Due to reasons beyond my control, I did not have the opportunity to socialize the concepts to the extent I would have liked. Consequently, with my team, I spent a lot of time during the project creating awareness of why we were doing the project and how the client would benefit. To effectively market the concept of SAP Fiori, as a minimum you should organize one-on-one overview sessions for key stakeholders and executives and webinars and brown-bag sessions for the potential users.

▶ Do not underestimate the effectiveness of a proof of concept. Some organizations are lukewarm to this idea because they feel it is not feasible and/or consider this throwaway work. While there is some truth to both arguments, it does not have to be that way. SAP has made the implementation of SAP Fiori apps quite quick (given the richness of the standard content). Therefore, you can easily use agile/scrum techniques. You have to disabuse your stakeholders of the notion that nothing in SAP can be rolled out quickly. As far as "throwaway" is concerned, if you treat your proof of concept as the initial implementation and are ready to invest accordingly in the SAP Fiori ecosystem at the outset, this is actually going to be your first productive SAP Fiori app. Therefore, I would strongly recommend the proof of concept route.

▶ Look at the possibility of using a rapid-deployment solution (RDS). In Chapter 7, I discussed SAP Fiori rapid-deployment solutions in detail. Adopting a rapid-deployment solution route could significantly reduce your time and effort by enabling you to leverage standard templates and best practices.

▶ Ensure that the IT organization understands that SAP Fiori requires a different set of skills than conventional SAP. I know of organizations that have viewed SAP Fiori through the lens of conventional SAP tools and technologies. Such organizations have scrambled to assemble the right resources. In Chapter 10, I discussed the skill sets necessary for supporting and enhancing SAP Fiori. These are quite different to your standard ABAP, SAP configuration type skill sets. This message has to be disseminated early on.

▶ Consider the security implications of implementing SAP Fiori at the outset. It is quite common for your client to be worried about the security of data in SAP transaction systems, especially since mobile devices will play a big role with SAP Fiori. Indeed, security has been the topic that most business stakeholders (especially those that are privy to financial data and personally identifiable information or PII) are most concerned about. You should consult with your client's in-house security specialist in detail before you write up the business case. Once your business case has been approved, the security specialist should be an integral part of your SAP Fiori deployment team. The areas that are typically relevant to most organizations are as follows: access through firewall (such as VPN access), single sign-on and authentication, and of course, roles and authorizations.

▶ It is presumptuous to approach your SAP Fiori business case from a pure cost-saving perspective. For a lot of technology professionals, especially those with a significant consulting background, there can hardly be a more compelling business proposition for your client than saving costs. However, as my own experiences have taught me, SAP Fiori as a product is more about providing users with a better overall experience that combines key characteristics such as simplicity, user-friendliness, intuitiveness, meaningful branding potential and superior navigation. Such attributes are qualitative—you would be hard-pressed to translate them into cost savings. The cost savings are likely to accrue over a long period of time (at least a year or so) once SAP Fiori becomes the standard SAP user interface for a majority of your organization's users. How? By leading to greater productivity as users spend less time navigating and making fewer clicks. Therefore, I would strongly recommend that you de-emphasize cost as a primary driver for an organization wanting to implement SAP Fiori.

▶ A key success factor for SAP Fiori (as with almost any new technology) is effective change management. By their very nature, new technologies are disruptive even though they are not meant to be so. However, it is entirely within the realm of human nature to eschew change and to hold onto the status quo no matter how welcome the change is. Once you have successfully completed your proof of concept and are ready to roll out SAP Fiori apps on a more widespread basis, you should identify the change agents that will not only champion SAP Fiori within the organization but also help with the transition from the conventional standard SAP user interface. I would recommend bringing in a professional organizational change manager who would create the strategy for effecting this change and work with the change agents to execute this change.

In this chapter, I shared with you various lessons learned and best practices involved in implementing SAP Fiori. I hope that you will be able to apply these in your respective organizations and maximize the benefits generated by SAP Fiori. We have now reached the end of our initial road trip with SAP Fiori. I hope you enjoyed the ride with me. Let the journey begin…

14 Resources and references

There is a lot of reference material available on SAP Fiori in the public domain. The following is a list of sources I feel are going to be really valuable in increasing your understanding of SAP Fiori:

- ▶ SAP Fiori portal on Help.sap.com: *https://help.sap.com/fiori*. This should be your starting point for official SAP Fiori information.

- ▶ An informative presentation on the evolution of SAP GUI: *https://prezi.com/gzx78ax-c1p1/evolution-of-sap-gui/*

- ▶ Complete and updated catalog of SAP apps: *http://help.sap.com/fiori_bs2013/helpdata/en/ed/e1e 153ddf60466e10000000a423f68/frameset.htm*

- ▶ Another (more) readable and consumable version of the SAP Fiori apps library with prerequisites and steps to get each SAP Fiori app up and running: *https://fioriappslibrary.hana.ondemand.com/sap/fix/e xternalViewer/*

- ▶ An easy to comprehend SAP Fiori installation guide: *https://blogs.sap.com/2016/12/07/sap-fiori-front-end-server-installation-guide/*

- ▶ SAP Fiori training courses and certification: *http://scn.sap.com/community/training-and-education/blog/2014/03/14/sap-education-introducing-new-sap-user-experience-education-portfolio-for-instructor-led-training-and-the-sap-learning-hub*

▶ SAP Fiori community on SAP's SDN site, containing blogs, posts, articles and other useful information on SAP Fiori:
http://scn.sap.com/community/fiori

▶ SAP Fiori design guidelines from SAP:
https://experience.sap.com/design-help/

▶ Information about SAP Screen Personas rapid deployment solution (RDS) on SAP's Enterprise Architecture Explorer site:
https://eaexplorer.hana.ondemand.com/_item.html ?id=11732#!/overview

▶ SAP user experience site containing important information and resources:
http://www.sap.com/solution/ux-user-experience/software/fiori/index.html

▶ SAP's comprehensive user experience website:
https://uxexplorer.hana.ondemand.com/_questions. html

▶ An interesting blog from 2014 on user experience (including both SAP Fiori and SAP Screen Personas) in light of the aborted SAP implementation at Avon:
http://www.forbes.com/sites/benkepes/2013/12/17/a vons-failed-sap-implementation-a-perfect-example-of-enterprise-it-revolution/

▶ A report covering SAP's announcement during Sapphire 2014 that they were going to make SAP Fiori free going forward:
http://www.cmswire.com/cms/information-management/now-you-can-now-have-sap-fiori-for-free-sapphirenow-025399.php#null

▶ Wiki link for SAP Screen Personas:
http://wiki.scn.sap.com/wiki/display/Img/SAPScreen Personas?original_fqdn=wiki.sdn.sap.com

- SAP Fiori Client on Android: *https://play.google.com/store/apps/details?id=com.sap.fiori.client&hl=en*

- SAP Fiori on Wikipedia: *http://en.wikipedia.org/wiki/SAP_Fiori*

- SAP Fiori Client for iOS devices in the Apple iTunes store: *https://itunes.apple.com/us/app/sap-fiori-client/id824997258?mt=8*

- SAP UI5 homepage: *http://www.sapui5.org/sapui5blogs/*

- Good blog on when to use the NetWeaver Business Client and when not to: *https://blogs.sap.com/2014/05/07/when-to-use-nwbc-and-when-you-really-shouldnt/*

- A very useful blog on SAP Fiori 2.0 entitled "SAP Fiori 2.0: The Ideal Overview": *https://experience.sap.com/skillup/sap-fiori-2-0-the-ideal-overview/*

- Links to the top 220 apps created in response to the SAP Fiori development challenge: *https://blogs.sap.com/2016/06/02/top-220-apps-created-from-the-sap-fiori-develop-challenge-now-on-scn/*

- Good blog on implementing SAP Fiori: *https://blogs.sap.com/2016/10/12/implementing-fiori-simplified-part-1/*

- A compilation of SAP Fiori blog posts: *http://fiori-implementation.com/blog/*

- Nice blog with hands-on guidance on how you can rapidly design and deploy your SAP Fiori apps using SAP Web IDE: *http://enterpriseplatformsblog.com/develop-your-mobile-app-on-the-cloud-sap/*

ESPRESSO TUTORIALS

You have finished the book.

Sign up for our newsletter!

Learn more about new e-books?

Get exclusive free downloads.

Sign up for our newsletter!

Please visit us at *newsletter.espresso-tutorials.com* to find out more.

A   The Author

Anurag Barua is an SAP expert and currently a Principal at TruQua Enterprises. He has 23 years of experience in conceiving, designing, managing, and implementing complex software solutions, including nearly18 years of experience with SAP applications. He has led multiple SAP implementations in various capacities. His core SAP competencies include FI and Controlling, Logistics, SAP HANA, SAP BW, SAP BusinessObjects, Enterprise Performance Management, SAP Solution Manager, SAP Fiori, Governance, Risk, and Compliance (GRC), and project management.

He is a frequent speaker at SAP conferences globally and contributes to several publications. He has written two books on SAP, including First Steps in Crystal Reports for Espresso Tutorials. He holds a Bachelor of Science in Computer Science and an MBA in Finance. He is a PMI-certified PMP, a Certified Scrum Master (CSM), and is ITIL V3F certified. You may contact Anurag via email at Anurag.barua@gmail.com.

B Index

C Disclaimer

This publication contains references to the products of SAP SE.

SAP, R/3, SAP NetWeaver, Duet, PartnerEdge, ByDesign, SAP BusinessObjects Explorer, StreamWork, and other SAP products and services mentioned herein as well as their respective logos are trademarks or registered trademarks of SAP SE in Germany and other countries.

Business Objects and the Business Objects logo, BusinessObjects, Crystal Reports, Crystal Decisions, Web Intelligence, Xcelsius, and other Business Objects products and services mentioned herein as well as their respective logos are trademarks or registered trademarks of Business Objects Software Ltd. Business Objects is an SAP company.

Sybase and Adaptive Server, iAnywhere, Sybase 365, SQL Anywhere, and other Sybase products and services mentioned herein as well as their respective logos are trademarks or registered trademarks of Sybase, Inc. Sybase is an SAP company.

SAP SE is neither the author nor the publisher of this publication and is not responsible for its content. SAP Group shall not be liable for errors or omissions with respect to the materials. The only warranties for SAP Group products and services are those that are set forth in the express warranty statements accompanying such products and services, if any. Nothing herein should be construed as constituting an additional warranty.

More Espresso Tutorials Books

Dominique Alfermann, Stefan Hartmann, Benedikt Engel:

SAP® HANA Advanced Modeling

► Data modeling guidelines and common test approaches

► Modular solutions to complex requirements

► Information view performance optimization

► Best practices and recommendations

http://5110.espresso-tutorials.com/

Christian Savelli:

SAP® BW on SAP HANA

► Tips for upgrading, maintaining, and running BW on HANA

► Data loading methods and real-time data acquisition

► New reporting paradigm for BW on HANA

► HANA data architecture

http://5128.espresso-tutorials.com

Janet Salmon & Claus Wild:

First Steps in SAP® S/4HANA Finance

▶ Understand the basics of SAP S/4HANA Finance

▶ Explore the new architecture, configuration options, and SAP Fiori

▶ Examine SAP S/4HANA Finance migration steps

▶ Assess the impact on business processes

http://5149.espresso-tutorials.com

Bert Vanstechelman:

The SAP® HANA Deployment Guide

▶ SAP HANA sizing, capacity planning guidelines, and data tiering

▶ Deployment options and data provisioning scenarios

▶ Backup and recovery options and procedures

▶ Software and hardware virtualization in SAP HANA

http://5171.espresso-tutorials.com

www.ingramcontent.com/pod-product-compliance
Lightning Source LLC
Chambersburg PA
CBHW071159050326
40689CB00011B/2183

* 9 7 8 1 5 1 2 0 4 1 3 4 7 *